Presented to:

my dear friend GERDA

From:

Ilse

Date:

Christmas 2004

> I have come that they may have life, and
> that they may have it more abundantly.
> John 10:10 NKJV

THE ABUNDANT *Life*

Solly Ozrovech

CHRISTIAN ART PUBLISHERS

Published in South Africa by Christian Art Publishers
PO Box 1599, Vereeniging, 1930

© 2004
First edition 2004

Compiled by Lynette Douglas from the following
devotionals by Solly Ozrovech:
The Glory of God's Grace
Intimate Moments with God
The Voice Behind You
New Beginnings
Fountains of Blessing

Cover designed by Christian Art Publishers

Scripture taken from the Holy Bible, New International Version®. NIV®
Copyright © 1973, 1978, 1984 by International Bible Society.
Used by permission of Zondervan Publishing House. All rights reserved.

Set in 14 on 16pt Palantino by Christian Art Publishers

Printed in China

ISBN 1-86920-401-8

© All rights reserved. No part of this book may be reproduced in
any form without permission in writing from the publisher, except
in the case of brief quotations in critical articles or reviews.

04 05 06 07 08 09 10 11 12 13 – 10 9 8 7 6 5 4 3 2 1

Dedication

I have come that they may have life, and that they may have it more abundantly. John 10:10 NKJV

Everybody longs for personal fulfillment, peace of mind, and true happiness. Unfortunately, many people do not achieve that because they fail to realize that our greatest fulfillment lies not in ourselves or in our possessions, but in glorifying God. It is only once we realize that we have been created by God and for God that we will discover meaning, purpose, and significance in our lives. Then we will bear fruit and so glorify God through an abundant life.

The Abundant Life is a celebration of Solly Ozrovech's 77th birthday, the more than seventy books that he has authored, and the innumerable readers around the world whose hearts he has touched with messages of hope and healing. It has been especially compiled from his previous devotionals to reflect on his many blessed years of wonderful writing.

Christian Art Publishers gratefully and proudly pays tribute to one of South Africa's most popular and gifted authors. We honor Solly Ozrovech's dedication and devotion to the Lord and the unequalled way in which he encourages and comforts millions of readers.

The Abundant Life is a treasure that aptly testifies to the author's life of fruitfulness, humility, grace, and abundance in Christ. May it bless and inspire every reader to claim Paul's assurance, *"God is able to make all grace abound to you, so that in all things at all times, having all that you need, you will abound in every good work"* (2 Corinthians 9:8).

~ The Publisher ~

January

Holy God, Creator of new things,
we thank You for the dawn of a new year.
Help us to discard the old ways of the old year
and to walk a new path in the new year,
to wait faithfully for Your blessing
in solemn and prayerful patience.
In the new year, through the strength
and mercy of God, which we have
experienced so often in the past,
we want to crucify the "own I" on the cross.
We pray that in this new year You would
grant us contentment with our lot,
so that we will look forward to each
new day with confidence, and venture
forth boldly with God at our side.
May Your bountiful blessings
accompany us in the new year.
May our path be strewn with many flowers
and may our joy as well as our grief
be hallowed by God.

~ Amen ~

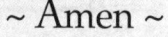

JANUARY 1

God is working through you

For it is God who works in you both to work and to will for his good purpose. (Phil. 2:13)

It is an overwhelming yet inspiring thought that God wants to work through us. God has a plan for your life and within the framework of that plan are those qualities that are needed to give full and perfect expression to the life God has given you.

You may be vaguely aware of your calling and destiny, yet the awareness might just not be strong enough to let you walk along the road that God has laid out for you. Therefore you live your life arbitrarily and not according to God's will.

However, if you acknowledge that God is truly at work within you, and if you obey Him in all things, God becomes your partner in the art of living. Then incredible things start to happen in your life. Obstructions either vanish or you approach them with strength and wisdom not of your own making. New prospects develop in your life, extending your vision and bitterness disappears. You are filled with inspiration and His plan unfolds more clearly as you move ahead, holding His hand.

God, in Your mercy, give me Your Holy Spirit to teach me Your way, and to lead me into the fullness of life that You have promised.

~ Amen ~

Experience the fullness of Christ

For God was pleased to have all his fullness dwell in him, and through him to reconcile to himself all things. (Col. 1:19-20)

It is not sufficient to maintain that Jesus was "a good person". That this is so is an irrefutable fact, accepted by all who have made a thorough study of His life. But He was more than "good": He was the epitome of perfection. Paul attempts to define the person of Christ by saying that *"God was pleased to have all His fullness dwell in Him"*.

This breathtaking truth is so overwhelming that we could hesitate to approach the Lord. But if He is your Savior, there is no barrier that can separate you from Him. Then John 10:10 becomes true in your life: *"I have come that they may have life, and have it to the full."* Then life becomes filled with fullness and festivity! At the beginning of this new year, read and meditate on Ephesians 3:17-18:

> So that Christ may dwell in your hearts through faith. And I pray that you, being rooted and established in love, may have power, together with all the saints, to grasp how wide and long and high and deep is the love of Christ.

I praise and glorify You, precious Lord, that, through faith, You abide in my heart. Make it a worthy abode.

~ Amen ~

Say "yes!" to life

"I have come that they may have life, and have it to the full." (Jn. 10:10)

The year ahead is a time of boundless opportunity to do good and to grow spiritually and intellectually. For you, the past may have been a tale of frustration and increasing bitterness, and you may feel that your life is void of inspiration and creativity.

But remember: the future belongs to you and you can do with it whatever you want to. God has given you freedom of choice. You can meet the future by being either positive or negative. The choice is yours.

Remember that every day is a gift from the loving hand of God, and you can only live life to the full when you yield yourself to God's purpose for your life.

The abundant life comes from God and, even though He is generous with this gift, He can only give it to those who are willing to receive and use it. Therefore, to say, "Yes!" to life is your privilege, as well as your responsibility.

Thank You that I have everlasting life because of Christ's crucifixion. Not even death can cause me to fear.

~ Amen ~

A quality life

"One's life does not consist in the abundance of the things he possesses." (Lk. 12:15)

Many people regard riches and possessions as crucial to their lives. They hoard things and compete with others trying to outdo their colleagues or rivals.

This lifestyle leads to tension, stress and unhappiness. It will definitely not lead to tranquility, peace of mind or fulfillment, because the obsession to hoard earthly treasures leads to the dangers of physical and mental illness.

True happiness, which leads to a life of abundant fulfillment, is only found through a real and meaningful relationship with the living Christ (see Jn. 10:10). It is when you live in and through Him that you partake of a life of true and constant abundance.

It is only when you commit yourself to the Master's service and decide to live according to His precepts that you realize true riches are to be found in the peace of mind and tranquility that He gives. It becomes your rich inheritance through your surrender to the Prince of Peace.

Addiction to earthly riches and possessions denigrates the quality of your life. Through Jesus Christ, God offers you a quality life – and it is free.

Divine Master, thank You that You have provided me with true riches, with the peace that passes all understanding through a meaningful relationship with You.

~ Amen ~

Live life to the full

"For with you is the fountain of life; in your light we see light." (Ps. 36:9)

If you want to lead a full and blessed life, there are certain principles that must be accepted. One of the most important is that you must be grateful for your life because it is the best thing God has given you. Of course this doesn't mean that everything will always be plain sailing, but when you accept the goodness of life, you will stop fighting against it.

When you accept that life is good, you become aware that it has a clear goal and plan. This acceptance removes all impatience and frustration, and life becomes an exciting and satisfying experience.

But in order for you to understand the great plan of life, you need to know the Planner. Accept the fact that God exists and allow your life to be controlled by godly principles, until eventually your life becomes an expression of those plans.

When you have this experience and make it your own, you possess a unity with the Creator and more and more your life is filled with the fullness of God. How can you possibly thank and praise Him enough for this in one lifetime?

Creator God, I thank You that You have a plan for my life that is filled with the fullness of You.

~ Amen ~

Fullness of life!

"I have come that they may have life, and that they may have it more abundantly." (Jn. 10:10)

Life is what you make of it. You can choose to be happy or miserable. The quality of your life depends on your own attitude and the way in which you approach and plan your life.

It is important that you look at your faith in the light of God's Word. In His Holy Scripture you will find numerous examples of people whose lives were once useless and empty, but who were transformed into inspired disciples. The condition is that you allow Jesus to reign in your life.

Christ specifically came that you may have life in abundance. Turn to Christ and walk your life's path in the company of the living Christ.

Like Paul and many others you will become a new creature in Christ. You will discover a new self-confidence and develop abilities that can only be received from the Holy Spirit.

Holy Spirit of God, I plead that You would help me to make decisions that lead to life and that bring joy to my life.

~ Amen ~

JANUARY 7

Life's most enriching experience

"Remain in me, and I will remain in you." (Jn. 15:4)

It is worth remembering that the stars are still shining, even when clouds hide them. Remember, too, that behind the dark patches of life the eternal love of your heavenly Father is still shining brightly. If you have cultivated trust in Him, your faith will carry you through the darkest moments of life. You will possess an inner peace and serenity that only He can give you.

When Jesus said, "Remain in me, and I will remain in you", He invited us to a noble lifestyle of which we could only dream before.

The life that He promises if we "remain in Him" is such a challenge that people hesitate to accept it and choose to stay in a religious rut that promotes neither joy nor spiritual growth.

The life that Christ promises is much more than an emotional experience. It creates inner peace, a constructive purpose in life, and provides the strength to achieve and maintain such a life through the power of the Holy Spirit.

Holy Father, I praise and glorify You for the life-changing strength that flows from the living Christ.

~ Amen ~

Reach for the sky!

I want to know Christ and the power of His resurrection ... becoming like Him in His death, and so, somehow, to attain to the resurrection from the dead. (Phil. 3:10-11)

Ambition is a commendable quality, as long as you do not become obsessed by it, and enslaved to it. Beware of fulfilling your ambitions at the expense of other people. Remember the words of Jesus: *"What good will it be for a man if he gains the whole world, yet forfeits his soul?"* (Mt. 16:26).

There is one goal in life that must surpass all others: to live in the image of Christ. This must be the greatest ambition of every follower of Jesus. It is, however, an ambition that demands complete surrender and commitment.

The pure joy of a life in Jesus Christ is beyond measure. Such a life is priceless and precious. It must, however, be remembered that the price of discipleship is sacrifice: sacrificing yourself, your thoughts, personal ambitions and dreams.

This might seem too high a price to pay, but as the triumphant resurrection followed the crucifixion of Jesus, so will the abundance of a life in Him, and through Him, be compensation for your complete surrender to your Savior and Redeemer.

Lord, I want to devote my entire life to Your service and to follow You wherever You may lead. Grant me the strength to do just that.

~ Amen ~

A life fulfilled in Christ

JANUARY 9

His divine power has given us everything we need for life and godliness through our knowledge of him who called us by his own glory and goodness. (2 Pet. 1:3)

Many people are dissatisfied with their lives. Some feel hurt and nurture bitterness and grievances in their hearts. These people tend to adopt a negative and defeatist attitude toward life and often withdraw from society and become lonely people.

They cease to enjoy life. It becomes a monotonous existence to them without any sense or meaning. Before long they find themselves without any friends.

If things are not going right for you at this moment, remember that you are a child of God and that He loves you dearly.

God, in His mercy, chose you to be His friend and He offers you the life-giving strength of the Holy Spirit to enable you to live life to the full.

Do not succumb to negative experiences and influences, but through Jesus Christ, rise above them and live your life the way He intended it to be.

Remember what Jesus said, *"I have come that they may have life, and have it to the full"* (Jn. 10:10).

I am lost in guilt. Only through You can I be born again. Thank You for forgiving my sins.

~ Amen ~

The truly abundant life

He who has the Son has life; he who does not have the Son of God does not have life. (1 Jn. 5:12)

People often say, "This is the life!" While we do not wish to undermine their enjoyment of what they have, it may, if left uncontrolled, lead to self-centeredness and hedonism. Such a seeking after pleasure often creates a sense of bored dissatisfaction and the need to seek out still other forms of sensual gratification. Eventually options for finding enjoyment run out and life becomes meaningless.

Whatever ways you choose to spend your leisure time, you must never lose sight of the fact that Jesus Christ came so that you may have life in abundance (see Jn. 10:10).

However satisfied you may feel in your work or relaxation, you will never be fully content until you have found the living Christ.

Don't limit your walk with Christ only to the spiritual things. He wants to be involved in every aspect of your life.

Invite Christ into your heart and allow Him to transform your existence into abundant life.

Redeemer and Master, since I have surrendered my life to You and allowed Your Spirit to rule my life, my fetters have fallen away and my heart has been liberated to live in abundance.

~ Amen ~

Abundant life

"He provides you with plenty of food and fills your hearts with joy." (Acts 14:17)

There are far too many people who feel that becoming a Christian will restrict their lives. They look at the lives of Christians and are not impressed by what they see. Why, they ask, should they get involved in a way of life that is restrictive, unattractive, and demanding?

If you look objectively at Christianity you will realize that the fault does not lie in the creed but in the way many people live out their faith.

It is unthinkable that the Creator of life will keep people from enjoying life; that He who is the epitome of beauty and perfection will want your life to be miserable and unattractive. He will not demand your love and then refuse to give you abundant life.

Christianity is a way of life that is filled with the abundance of God through Jesus Christ.

When the objective of your life is to reflect the glory of Christ, your life will overflow with joy and peace.

My sincere prayer is, O Lord, that my life will reflect Your glory more and more through the work of the Holy Spirit in me.

~ Amen ~

Life in all its fullness

That you may be filled to the measure of all the fullness of God. (Eph. 3:19)

There are people who allege that life is empty and futile and that it is not worthwhile to carry on living. They have lost interest in life and in the fullness that life has to offer.

While we will experience setbacks in life, which at times rock the foundations of our very existence, we must never lose sight of Jesus. He came so that we can have abundant life (see Jn. 10:10). He assures us that, in every situation, He will be with us (see Mt. 28:20). He promised that He would carry our burden with us (see Mt. 11:28-30). The only requirement is that we must turn to Him in faith.

If you are depressed you need to enter into an intimate relationship with the living Christ by means of prayer and meditation. Share your doubts and your fears with Him.

Remember that the Bible says, *"Cast all your anxiety on him because he cares for you"* (1 Pet. 5:7). Then through God's great grace you will find meaning and direction for your life.

Lord, Your blessings fall down on me like soft rain. You gladden my heart. Grant me the fullness of Your Spirit.

~ Amen ~

JANUARY 13

Make something of your life

But one thing I do: Forgetting what is behind and straining toward what is ahead. (Phil. 3:13)

The people who achieve success in life choose their goals and strive to achieve them with unremitting zeal. They dedicate themselves to the fulfillment of their ideals.

Ensure that your goals are worthy of the best that is in you. You will never find satisfaction in life if you aim too low.

Some people aspire to excel in the academic world, others in business or the arts. Regardless of the sphere in which you move, you must live life to the full. If you are a disciple of Jesus, you should want to leave the world a better place than you found it.

The highest goal that you can aspire to is to become like Christ. This may sound too idealistic to be practically possible, but such a goal reflects true wisdom. Christ calls you to the most exalted life possible.

However, not only does He call you, He also enables you to achieve heights that you never would have reached in your own strength. Make your life worthwhile through the strength of your Master.

Through Your presence in me, Lord Jesus, I will achieve the goals that You have placed in my heart.

~ Amen ~

Find joy in the small things

For everything God created is good, and nothing is to be rejected if it is received with thanksgiving, because it is consecrated by the word of God and prayer. (1 Tim. 4:4-5)

Many of us tend to take things for granted. This is an unfortunate attitude, because it distorts our ability to appreciate the intrinsic value of things. The colors of the flowers, the song of the birds, the beauty of a sunrise or sunset are all things that many people barely notice.

It is only when you begin to contemplate a life without these blessings that you begin to realize how drab and mediocre your existence would become. Life without these gifts of God would be colorless and uninteresting.

We should cherish and appreciate every blessing in our lives, be it large or small. We should learn to appreciate the wonders of God's creation because it adds meaning, beauty and purpose to our lives.

We should appreciate everything that God has granted us in His grace, but we should also realize that we have an obligation to carefully protect and conserve the wonders of creation. This is the most practical way of thanking God for His greatness and benevolence.

Heavenly Father, I thank You for the everyday things in my life and for everything that they mean to me.

~ Amen ~

Are you a workaholic?

January 15

In vain you rise early and stay up late, toiling for food to eat – for he grants sleep to those he loves. (Ps. 127:2)

There are many people who are addicted to their work. They allow their work to control every area of their lives. The usual result is that they have little time for their families or for leisure activities. This inevitably leads to a breakdown in health, a disintegration of family, and a distortion of the meaning of life.

Of course God does expect Christians to work hard and with dedication and integrity so that He will be glorified through the way that we do our work. But He also expects us to set aside time to rest and relax so that we can return to our work refreshed and strengthened and able to fulfill our potential.

In order to balance work and play, Christ needs to be at the center of our lives. Develop a sensitivity to the voice of the Holy Spirit in your life and let Him help you to give work and rest their proper places in your schedule.

You will find that God will abundantly supply all your needs as you obey Him and live according to His will.

Please make me reliable in my daily tasks, O Lord, yet let me follow the example of Jesus and make time to rest and become quiet before You.

~ Amen ~

Share your burdens with Christ

JANUARY 16

Cast all you anxiety on him because he cares for you.
(1 Pet. 5:7)

A businessman who was going through a difficult time was asked how he managed to sleep with all the worries that he had. He answered that he relinquished all his problems to God, saying, *"Indeed, he who watches over Israel will neither slumber nor sleep"* (Ps. 121:4), and he saw no point in both of them staying awake all night.

Jesus promised never to abandon or forsake us (see Heb. 13:5). He invited those who are weary and overburdened to come to Him for rest.

This does not mean that all your problems will disappear simply because you pray. It does mean that if you place your faith and trust in God and confide in Him in prayer, you will experience the peace of mind that will sensitize you to the guidance of the Holy Spirit.

In His strength you will be able to handle your problems in accordance with the will of God.

Soothe my restless heart, O Holy Spirit. Calm the tempestuous ocean and the storms that rage. Lead me to waters where there is serenity so that I can experience peace of mind.

~ Amen ~

JANUARY 17

Without God you have nothing

"What good will it be for a man if he gains the whole world, yet forfeits his soul? Or what can a man give in exchange for his soul?" (Mt. 16:26)

From our childhood years onwards we dream about what we want to become and what we want to do, and those dreams determine the quality of our lives. You can continue dreaming and allow the years to slip by while not achieving anything worthwhile. Or your dreams could inspire you to take action.

It is important that the dream that inspires you is big enough to present a challenge. If your dreams limit you to gathering earthly treasures, to living a meaningless social life, you are doing yourself a great injustice.

Remember that you have been created in the image of God and He has destined you for far greater things.

Develop a growing awareness of God's presence in your everyday life. Don't let the material things around you detract from the power and beauty of the living God. Earthly treasures should not be more important to you than the things of God. Turn to God and determine to live according to His standards then your life will become truly meaningful.

Remember: Without God you have nothing!

Thank You, Father, that I can inherit Your kingdom. Thank You for blessing me in ways that leave me speechless.

~ Amen ~

Live fully!

And we pray this in order that you may live a life worthy of the Lord and may please him in every way: bearing fruit in every good work, growing in the knowledge of God. (Col. 1:10)

People these days seem to be constantly bored and dissatisfied with life. But God's promise to you is – and always has been – that He will give you life, and that in abundance. There are no limits to the quality of life that Jesus Christ offers to you. Every moment of His life on earth was filled with purpose and meaning, and in everything He did the will of the Father and brought glory and honor to His name.

By the grace of God and through the power of the Holy Spirit in you, God expects you to live a similar kind of life – right here and now. Renew your mind as you study the eternal Word of God and renew your soul as you spend time in prayer and meditation.

Come into His holy presence often and let Him fill your life with new purpose, new goals and new joy.

Let your attitude be the same as that of Jesus. Fulfill His will and obey Him in all things and your life will yield a rich harvest that will glorify God.

Perfect Example and Redeemer, through You I rejoice in the blessed knowledge that I can experience true life in all its richness and fullness.

~ Amen ~

A life of victory

JANUARY 19

For everyone born of God overcomes the world. This is the victory that has overcome the world, even our faith.
(1 Jn. 5:4)

Perhaps life is an ongoing struggle for you. Everything you undertake seems to end up in frustration and failure. This knocks your self-confidence so that you shrink back from new endeavors and start falsely believing that nothing you ever do will succeed.

Self-pity eats away at your belief in yourself and in what you can achieve. And so you become your own worst enemy. Self-pity creates self-centeredness and blocks your ability to find the purpose and meaning of true life.

The only way to avoid self-inflicted limitations is to submit to the discipline of faith. Faith will inspire you and help you to see beyond yourself. You develop a deeper and broader perspective on life. It enables you to acknowledge that it is only through the strength and influence of the living Christ, through the Holy Spirit that lives in you, that you can constructively deal with problems and failures. Through faith in Christ you can live on conquered ground from day to day.

Holy Master, I thank You that I can live victoriously because I believe that You are my Savior and that the Holy Spirit lives in me. I thank You for every victory that I win over myself.

~ Amen ~

Into the future with Christ

JANUARY 20

"Be strong and courageous. Do not be terrified; do not be discouraged, for the Lord your God will be with you." (Josh. 1:9)

We usually enter the new year with mixed feelings. Aware of the failures of the past, we face the future with some hesitation. What the new year holds will depend largely on you. You can sidestep its challenges and continue in the same old rut you have been in for many years. Or you can grab the opportunities that come your way, and develop a completely new lifestyle and approach to life.

There are two ways of handling the challenges of the new year. You can approach them as before, wanting to do better, but convinced that you will be back in the same old rut of unfulfilled expectations and miserable failures before the end of January.

Or you can meet the new year with the conviction that you serve a wonderful God who desires only victory and fulfillment for you.

God offers you not only the gifts and grace of a disciplined spiritual life, but also the privilege of being His child through Jesus Christ. Trust Jesus and put your faith in Him, and the new year will be filled with joy and peace.

Holy Lord Jesus, because You have given me Your Spirit, I can face the future with courage and confidence. For this I praise and thank You from the bottom of my heart.

~ Amen ~

JANUARY 21

Attempt great things

He is your praise, and he is your God, who has done for you these great and awesome things which your eyes have seen. (Deut. 10:21)

Many people live their lives based on what others think of them. Because society expects little from them, they expect little from themselves. But at times they become aware of deep, strange stirrings in their spirit because each of us has a portion of the life-giving breath of God in them.

As you become aware of this you will start searching for broader spiritual and mental horizons. You will be dissatisfied with your present situation and yearn for a meaningful future.

But often, while you long to move ahead, inspired by these new insights, there are things in your life that hold you back. It might feel as though you cannot escape your past and so you retreat into your old life with crumbled hopes and shattered dreams.

If God has given you a vision, then you can be sure it will require effort and hard work. Only if you accept the challenge and trust God will you be able to find out what you are really able to do.

My Lord, I pray that You would help me to discover the full plan You have for my life and that through Your strength I can become all You created me to be.

~ Amen ~

God's abundance

So that they may have the full riches of complete understanding, in order that they may know the mystery of God, namely Christ, in whom are hidden all the treasures of wisdom and knowledge. (Col. 2:2-3)

Many people are unaware of the immeasurable generosity of God. Their own needs and dire poverty blind them to the One who could transform their poverty into abundance, if only they accept Him as their Savior, and obey Him.

Scripture teaches us that God is much more willing to give than we are to receive. If we pray in faith we will receive what we pray for.

We know that God is able to do everything we ask, but we also see the obstacles that we place in the way of His answers. If you bring a request to your heavenly Father, make sure you don't harbor doubt in your heart.

The way God answers your prayers is neither your concern nor your responsibility. A simple, childlike faith which looks to God, believing steadfastly that He does answer prayer, gladdens His heart and elicits a response. God hears your prayers and will meet your every need from His treasure house – according to His glorious grace.

Holy Spirit, thank You for Your great generosity and kindness to me.

~ Amen ~

JANUARY 23

The secret of a joyful life

Always give thanks to God the Father for everything, in the name of our Lord Jesus Christ. (Eph. 5:20)

If Christ abides in you through faith you become more aware of the beauty and splendor of your fellowmen, as well as in the world around you. The greater your appreciation, the more life will reveal its hidden treasures to you.

As the prophet says, Jesus came, *"To comfort all who mourn, and provide for those who grieve in Zion – to bestow on them a crown of beauty instead of ashes, the oil of gladness instead of mourning, and a garment of praise instead of a spirit of despair"* (Is. 61:2-3).

When you read the Scriptures, you cannot miss the continuous, resounding, triumphant note of gratitude. It is simply an expression of appreciation towards God for all His blessings.

He is infinitely patient and His dealings with us are so merciful. How can we not appreciate all the good things that He gives us?

We are closest to God when we praise and glorify Him. Then He becomes a reality in our lives and our lives become an ongoing celebration.

Thank You, Lord Jesus, that You have given me a heart that is grateful for Your love and gifts.

~ Amen ~

Where are you going?

JANUARY 24

"Thanks be to God, who always leads us in triumphal procession in Christ." (2 Cor. 2:14)

Some people seem to achieve success with seeming ease, while others are plagued by defeat. To ascribe this to coincidence would be contrary to the law of cause and effect. Nothing happens by chance – at least not in the lives of God's children.

It is not always easy to choose which road you should follow. But accepting Christ as Lord of your life puts divine powers into action. Your values in Him will provide you with an inspired yet practical goal.

Choosing your goal with Christ's guidance is the highest form of common sense. It implies cooperation with God that is the result of His tremendous blessing in your life.

Choosing your objectives with Christ's help puts your feet on a road that you can follow with a clear conscience. It will bring joy, confidence and enthusiasm into your life. A by-product of this choice is that the relationship between you and the triune God becomes more intimate on a daily basis. If you walk through life in the light of God, the whole journey becomes a joyous experience.

Dear Guide, thank You that I can choose to walk through life with You, and that You guide me along the paths of life.

~ Amen ~

JANUARY 25

Reach your goal

And observe what the LORD your God requires: Walk in his ways, and keep his decrees and commands, his laws and requirements, as written in the Law of Moses, so that you may prosper in all you do and wherever you go. (1 Kgs. 2:3)

Every person wants to successfully achieve his ambitions and goals. There are few people, if any, who can honestly say that success doesn't mean anything to them; that they will be satisfied, regardless of what happens to them in life. Life would be empty and meaningless for the person with no goals or ambition.

But for those who have a passionate desire to succeed, failure could be a bitter pill to swallow. It can deal a serious blow to their confidence. Many people give up because they despair of ever obtaining success. Every disappointment or failure is a destructive blow to their ambition.

It is important that you should accept the fact that it is impossible to be successful through only your own abilities. You need Jesus Christ's guidance and support to help you make the right decisions. If the living Christ is your partner in life, then you can rest assured that everything you do will bring a deep and lasting sense of fulfillment.

Holy Spirit, please help me to stay on course and to achieve success in all that You have called me to do.

~ Amen ~

Presented to:

_____

From:

_____

Date:

_____

The reassuring presence of Christ

Jesus himself stood among them and said to them, "Peace be with you." (Lk. 24:36)

After the terrible events of the first Good Friday, Jesus' followers were stunned. Without their beloved Master they were scared, confused and without a leader. Their dreams had been shattered and life had lost all meaning. All their hopes and expectations were destroyed when they saw the One they believed was the Messiah humiliated by His shameful death. This disheartened group were commiserating together – when Jesus suddenly appeared in their midst.

The transformation in their lives was nothing short of a miracle. The Scriptures abound with examples of the mighty deeds that they performed in the Name of the Master. The presence of Jesus brought new impetus to their lives.

The resurrected, living Christ still has the same impact on the lives of people today. If you are disheartened; if you have given up hope; when problems threaten to become too much; then invite Jesus into your life and ask Him to care for you. Trust Him unconditionally and allow Him to change your despair into hope and your sadness into joy.

I ask You, beloved Redeemer, to send Your Holy Spirit to change my life so that I will constantly be aware of Your holy presence.

~ Amen ~

A gracious signpost

Who, then, is the man that fears the LORD? He will instruct him in the way chosen for him. He will spend his days in prosperity, and his descendants will inherit the land. (Ps. 25:12-13)

Our lives can become extremely complicated, especially in these modern times when so many people find themselves caught in a maze and see no way out. Many people cannot handle such situations and they are tossed to and fro like driftwood across the sea of life. Their lives are controlled by the storms, the tides and the winds and sometimes, to their great relief, the calm.

Your life follows this pattern only if you allow it to. God will accompany you along the way that He has ordained for you, if you obediently follow Him. Initially it may seem as if the things that happen to you are not in your best interests, but when you see the end result you will realize that God's way is always best.

Lay every decision that you have to make, whether big or small, before Jesus Christ in prayer. Share your life with the living Christ in the knowledge that He will guide you along a safe path – a path that He has already walked and that He will make clear to you through grace.

I praise You, Lord, that I can follow You knowing that You lead me along the best way for my life.

~ Amen ~

God performs His wonders through you

Cast all your anxiety on him because he cares for you.
(1 Pet. 5:7)

You may be concerned about your job or your co-workers, about an increase in taxes or rent, or about the conduct of a loved one. You see only gloom and an unsure future. When your life is paralyzed by fear, you cannot experience the freedom and joy that God offers to those who love and trust Him.

If you are anxious and worried, remember that God is greater than everything that happens to you. Clouds of anxiety, fear and uncertainty might currently obscure your image of God, but He is always constant.

With thanksgiving, take your anxieties, fears and worries and share them with your merciful God. Give these things over to Him unreservedly. Accept the challenge to follow God's plan of action. God's omnipotence will sweep away all irrelevant thoughts, and all uncertainty will disappear. The true greatness of God is not only revealed in His majestic universe, but also in His immeasurable love and concern for people like you and me.

Your works are perfect, Lord and, even when I drink from the cup of bitterness, You will never forsake me, but You will help me to understand eventually that with You, I will live forever.

~ Amen ~

Power from on high

FEBRUARY 28

"But you will receive power when the Holy Spirit comes on you; and you will be my witnesses in Jerusalem, and in all Judea and Samaria, and to the ends of the earth." (Acts 1:8)

Many well-meaning Christians never develop their full potential because they don't understand the person and work of the Holy Spirit. And so they are not able to serve Christ as effectively as they want to.

If you depend on your own strength in your service to the Master, you are sure to fail. This kind of service can never be effective. Jesus Himself said, *" ... apart from me you can do nothing"* (Jn. 15:5).

You cannot earn His presence or serve Him in your own strength. The anointing is a gift of grace given to you when you submit to the authority of the living Christ and when you pray diligently. Willingly receive the blessing and the privilege and the responsibility of this gift.

Do not expect your experience to be the same as someone else's as the gifts of the Spirit can manifest differently in your life.

Accept God's gift with gratitude and joy, and allow the Spirit to lead you into the service that He has chosen for you. Then serve Him with faith, boldness and peace.

Holy Lord, reveal Yourself to me through Your Spirit so that Your kingdom will rule and reign in my life.

~ Amen ~

Together with God

I can do everything through him who gives me strength.
(Phil. 4:13)

When you think of God in all His divine glory and of yourself as an insignificant little speck on the planet earth, it becomes incredibly difficult to identify yourself with Him. Despite this, the Holy Spirit dwells in your spirit. Realizing this releases a powerful force in your life. It is God's will for you to have a vibrant and living relationship with Him.

When you realize that God reveals Himself in and through you, you will experience strength, balance and dynamism in your life. And you will develop a strong sense of responsibility. When you realize that God created you and that His Spirit lives in you, you will no longer live to please yourself, but rather to do His will. Through the grace of God you can attain this kind of life in the strength of the Lord Jesus Christ.

Before our Savior ascended to heaven He promised that His Spirit would be with those who accept Him as Savior and Lord and who are willing to allow His Spirit to work through them.

Merciful Lord Jesus, I accept the gift of the Holy Spirit and therefore enjoy intimate communion with You, my Lord and my God.

~ Amen ~

March

Lord, I rejoice that I can bring
all my problems to You in prayer.
I praise You because through prayer my
relationship with You flourishes.
You taught us to say, "Abba! Father!"
so that we can draw close to God,
as a little child comes to his father.
Thank You for the glorious privilege
of being able to talk to You
under any circumstances, knowing
that You hear and answer.
I glorify and praise Your Name,
because I can bring all things to You in prayer,
and You will provide all that I truly need.
You know what is best for me.
I rest in Your holy will.
It is wonderful to know that
there are always new mysteries in prayer,
waiting to be discovered.
Therefore, I humbly ask
with Your disciples of old:
"Lord, teach us to pray!"

~ Amen ~

MARCH 1

Effective prayer

Jesus went out to a mountainside to pray, and spent the night praying to God. (Lk. 6:12)

Nobody can grow spiritually without a continually developing prayer life. The Lord showed us the importance of long periods of time alone with God. Our faith can only be effective if we have a pulsating prayer life.

Christians should have an overwhelming desire to pray. Yet, very often prayer is the step-child of spiritual growth instead of being its foundation. Your prayer life can only be effective to the extent that you are praying.

Prayer requires strict discipline and regular application. There are times that you realize the importance of prayer, but perhaps are not really in the mood for it. In actual fact it is when you don't feel like praying at all that you should persevere. If your prayer life is impoverished, you are the only person responsible for that.

Make sure that all your prayers are focused on God. Many prayers seem to accentuate the problem, instead of praising God for His ability to deal with it.

Lord, You who answers prayers, help me to pray more fervently, more effectively.

~ Amen ~

Come, let us pray

And there on the beach we knelt to pray. (Acts 21:5)

There are also people who believe that prayer should be limited to the church or to the privacy of your inner room. They regard any form of public prayer in the course of daily life with uneasiness or even disapproval.

Prayer is as much a form of communication as is conversation. The difference is merely that conversation is a form of communication between people, while prayer is a conversation between us and our heavenly Father. There is nothing more natural than this.

There are moments in our lives when it is both essential and desirable to draw near to God. Then prayer is normal and appropriate.

While you should never be too shy to pray, it is also necessary to be discreet in terms of the time and the place you choose to pray. Trust in the guidance of the Holy Spirit and your prayers will at all times be a blessing to you as well as others.

O Hearer of prayers, thank You that I can draw near to Your sacred throne at all times and under all circumstances, and know that You will always listen.

~ Amen ~

MARCH 3

The sound of silence

And after the fire came a gentle whisper. (1 Kgs. 19:12)

We live in a time of deafening din and noise. Radios, "muzak" and CD players bombard us with their noise wherever we go. Some music is pleasing and soothing, but much of the noise that passes as "music" is stressful on the ears. Because we have become used to noise, we no longer know how to deal with silence. When surrounded by silence, we become restless and look for something to fill the gap.

To enjoy and appreciate silence is one of the great joys in life. It is then that your spirit becomes receptive to the presence of God. If you fellowship with God in silence, you will be able to face life with self-confidence and dignity.

Enter the silence with a prayer that the Holy Spirit will fill your thoughts with good things. Meditate on the Lord's omnipotence, majesty, or the beauty of His creation. When you are alone with God in silence and you become aware of His living presence, your time of quiet reflection becomes a time of spiritual empowerment and inspiration.

Lord, I will wait upon You in quiet trust. I know that You will strengthen my faith. You guarantee that through the blood of Christ.

~ Amen ~

The miraculous power of praise

My heart is steadfast, O God; I will sing and make music with all my soul. Awake, harp and lyre! I will awaken the dawn. (Ps. 108:1-2)

We often use prayer to thank God for what He has done for us, to lay our needs before Him, and to confess our sins and shortcomings to Him. It is sad, but true, that we often neglect to express our praise of Him in prayer.

Never underestimate the power of praise in your prayer life. If someone impresses you, you praise him. Good artists, sportsmen, musicians and singers are showered with praise.

Why shouldn't we then shower the benevolent God with praise? Think of all the remarkable things that He has done; the miracles that flow from Him; the extraordinary extent of His love. Ponder for a moment the wonders of the universe and creation; of human life and achievement – and praise and glorify Him. More than anyone He is worthy of our love and thanksgiving.

If you concentrate on praising and glorifying God, you will create a very special relationship with the living Christ, which will transform your prayer life and intensify your love for Him.

Great and wonderful God, we want to exalt Your name, and praise and glorify You for all the wonders of Your love and grace that You give to us.
~ Amen ~

Integrity before God

I know, my God, that you test the heart and are pleased with integrity. (1 Chr. 29:17)

If you sincerely cultivate a positive and meaningful prayer life, you will at some time or another experience the problem of wandering thoughts.

In the time you set aside to be alone with your heavenly Father you may read a passage from the Bible or from an inspirational book. Then you start praying, only to discover that instead of being focused on God, your thoughts run amok and start focusing on the most irrelevant or even profane things.

If this has happened to you, take comfort in the thought that it happens to everyone who takes prayer seriously. However, those who have persevered have ultimately succeeded in making their prayers a delightful and powerful force in their lives.

When your thoughts wander, don't become upset or frustrated. Simply turn your thoughts back to God, and ask the Holy Spirit to take control of your mind.

The problem of wandering thoughts can be conquered, so don't allow it to spoil your relationship with the living Christ.

Thank You, heavenly Lord, that I can experience the reality of Your living presence through prayer. For this I praise Your name.

~ Amen ~

An effective prayer life

Do not be anxious about anything, but in everything, by prayer and petition, with thanksgiving, present your requests to God. (Phil. 4:6)

Of all the Christian disciplines, prayer is probably most commonly practiced and least understood. So many people regard prayer as a life-jacket to be used in desperate situations, when everything else has failed. Or as a way to tell God what they really want, or to obtain His blessing for something they have already decided to do. No wonder so many people claim that their prayers go unanswered.

We need to begin by establishing a relationship of prayer with God. Develop an understanding of the living Christ by constantly acknowledging His presence in your daily life. Grow closer to Him by studying His Word, and meditate in the quiet presence of God.

Thank and praise God for the privilege of prayer, and then cast all your cares, fears, problems and requests on Him and ask Him to grant you what He knows you need, and the grace to handle any situation that might arise. Then wait patiently on Him and be sensitive to the whisperings of the Holy Spirit. Then God's plan will unfold itself in your life.

You grant us more than we could ever ask for. We always have the blessed assurance of Your love and know that Your promises hold good.

~ Amen ~

Prayer is the key

MARCH 7

My purpose is that they may be encouraged in heart and united in love, so that they may have the full riches of complete understanding, in order that they may know the mystery of God, namely, Christ, in whom are hidden all the treasures of wisdom and knowledge. (Col. 2:2-3)

Many Christians are ignorant of God's boundless grace. Their need blinds them to the One who could supply their need if they would only trust Him.

Time and again Scripture reiterates that God is more willing to give than we are to receive. We are constantly reminded that if we pray and believe we will receive that which we pray for. Prayer is the key which unlocks the treasure chambers of God.

God's believing children know that He can do anything that we ask, but many of us also erect our own barriers that obstruct His answers. When you bring a petition before God, don't start thinking how unlikely it is that God will answer your prayer because there are so many obstacles in the way.

How God is going to answer your prayers is neither your responsibility nor your concern. A simple, child-like faith that looks to God and believes unconditionally that He does answer prayer is the kind of prayer that God wants to answer with joy.

I thank You for the key of prayer with which we can unlock the precious treasure house of Your blessings.

~ Amen ~

An exercise in prayer

Be joyful in hope, patient in affliction, faithful in prayer.
(Rom. 12:12)

Is your prayer life everything you want it to be? Is it all that Christ would like it to be? Your answer can make the difference between an ineffective prayer life or one that is filled with an awareness of the presence of God.

While you are praying you undoubtedly pray for your family and friends and it is possible that you seldom think beyond them. Yet the whole world cries out for prayer.

Every newspaper is a prayer manual. Pray for the editors and those who form public opinion; pray for those who grieve; for the victims of violence; even for those who committed the acts of violence. You may even be able to find something for which to thank God.

Give some thought in prayer to those who seem tired and disillusioned or to all the irritable people you encounter. Rejoice together with those who are happy and thank God for their happiness. You never have to search for a reason to pray.

While you are praying for others you will develop a more intimate communion with the living Christ.

Lord Jesus, with Your disciples I want to ask: Teach me to pray!

~ Amen ~

MARCH 9

The challenge of true prayer

"And when you pray, do not be like the hypocrites, for they love to pray standing in the synagogues and on the street corners to be seen by men. I tell you the truth, they have received their reward in full." (Mt. 6:5)

Personal prayer has many facets. It is a wonderful source of comfort. Once you are aware of the tremendous power of prayer you will find that your view of life will expand. Personal prayer enables you to remain calm in the midst of life's storms. The rewards of cultivating a positive prayer life are many and varied.

There is, however, one facet of prayer that is very often overlooked. I'm referring to those times when God wants to reveal to you His will and desires for your life.

Often God's expectations are at variance with your own desires. You would much rather not listen to what God wants to say to you.

If, however, you have the courage to persevere in prayer, not only will His will be revealed to you, but you will also develop a new goal for your life – and together with that the peace of God, which guarantees you peace of mind.

Your expectations are contrary to my desires. Please help me to discern Your will and to pray according to Your plans.

~ Amen ~

Pray – regardless ...

"When my life was ebbing away, I remembered you, Lord, and my prayer rose to you, to your holy temple." (Jon. 2:7)

Many people deny themselves the privilege of the peace of God simply because they feel too undeserving to talk to God. When in despair, they will not draw near to the throne of mercy because they have not previously spent much time in the presence of the Lord. Others are overwhelmed by feelings of guilt or shame and they hesitate to draw near to God in prayer. Whatever the reason, they deprive themselves of the peace of God, which surpasses all understanding.

Jesus promised that He will not cast out anybody who comes to Him. He also emphasized that He came not to call the righteous, but sinners to salvation. Throughout the Scriptures you can read of His unfathomable mercy and endless love that reach out to all people: the good and the bad, the worthy and the unworthy.

It is never too late for you to turn to the one who answers all prayers. He will always hear your desperate call and cover you with His love. However unworthy you may feel, reach out to Him in prayer and He will take you by the hand.

Father, I want to live my whole life glorifying You. Help me not to lose sight of You when times are difficult.

~ Amen ~

MARCH 11

The path of prayer

"And when you pray, do not keep on babbling like pagans, for they think they will be heard because of their many words ... for your Father knows what you need before you ask him." (Mt. 6:7-8)

Repetitive prayers may be a good way to develop the spirit of prayer, but the Lord makes it abundantly clear that prayer becomes ineffective when it deteriorates into the mere recital of pretty phrases.

True prayer is more than words. It is an attitude of the spirit and mind that reaches out to the eternal God. When you pray you must be willing to be used by God to answer your own prayers. Too often we lay our needs before Him and then disappear from the scene, instead of being sensitive to hearing and obeying His voice. Prayer is a two-way process. You tell God what you want from Him and He reveals to you what He expects from you.

Prayer is not a series of empty words that are divorced from real life, but rather an increasingly intimate relationship with the heavenly Father and a sincere desire to do His will. When He reveals His will to you, you will be inspired to offer the kind of praise and worship that will enrich the quality of your life.

God and Father, grant me the true spirit of prayer so that my communion with You will become more and more profound and meaningful.

~ Amen ~

The gracious gift of prayer

Devote yourselves to prayer, being watchful and thankful. (Col. 4:2)

What value do you place on prayer? Do you regard it as a very special gift of grace from God, or as an almost unbearable burden? When some people move into the presence of God in prayer, they experience what the hymn writer described as being "lost in wonder, love and praise".

Sadly the great majority of Christians regard prayer as an unpleasant task that needs to be done. And so they pretend to pray, but all they actually do is repeat well-known phrases like a meaningless recitation.

The privilege of prayer is a very special gift of grace from God. It is God's personal invitation to you to enter into His sanctuary and to talk to Him and listen when He has something to say to you.

Prayer is a discipline that requires preparation and practice. Make time to come quietly into the presence of God. Focus your attention on Jesus. Listen to God as well as speak to Him, thanking Him for the gracious gift of His strength for you. That will enable you to live in an atmosphere of peace and trust.

Thank You for the privilege of being able to bring every aspect of my life to You in prayer.

~ Amen ~

MARCH 13

Spiritual growth through prayer

After Job had prayed for his friends, the LORD made him prosperous again and gave him twice as much as he had before. (Job 42:10)

It is not hard to make enemies. You only have to say the wrong thing, or even do absolutely nothing, and you will find that you have somehow managed to make an enemy. No one enjoys making enemies.

Remember that it is possible to turn an enemy into a friend. Granted, this isn't always easy, because forgiveness requires true greatness. Trying to understand the false pride, secret fears and plain foolishness of that person may help in this process. But only those who have undergone meaningful spiritual growth can transform enmity into friendship.

Those who are spiritually stunted keep the glowing embers of bitterness burning in their attitudes, words and deeds.

One sure and practical way of starting to turn enemies into friends is by praying for them. To many of us this may sound absurd, but it is a truly wise act if you desire a pleasant life. Prayer changes your attitude toward people and events, and when this happens, the battle is just about won. With God on your side, you will have the ultimate victory.

Dear Lord, help me to grow in You so that I may develop a forgiving spirit. You have forgiven me through Your grace. Help me to follow Your example.

~ Amen ~

Prayer is boundless

MARCH 14

At Gibeon the LORD appeared to Solomon during the night in a dream, and God said, "Ask for whatever you want me to give you." (1 Kgs. 3:5)

Many people get irritated with verbose people who come with long-winded requests. They obscure the real issue behind a flood of words instead of making a straightforward request. They then lose sight of their need and confuse the person at whom the request is directed, because it is so unclear.

A similar situation can arise in your prayer life. Are you really totally open and clear about your needs when you come before God? A study of the psalms and prayers in the Old Testament clearly shows that the prayer-warriors of old were completely open and honest when they spoke with the Lord. They did not hide or hold back anything. Their confessions were complete and revealing, their requests were real and humble.

When presenting your requests to the Lord, be specific, without being too demanding. Offer your prayers to Him in faith and accept His divine will for your life. Ask for the gifts of wisdom and discernment so that you can recognize and accept His answers – and wait patiently on the Lord.

I want to be completely open when I speak to You about the situations I am facing today. I cannot face them without Your wisdom and discernment. Please help me to do what is right and best.

~ Amen ~

MARCH 15

Wisdom comes through prayer

If any of you lacks wisdom, he should ask God, who gives generously to all without finding fault; and it will be given to him. (Jas 1:5)

Many people think prayer is a spiritual excuse for those who lack the courage to face the challenges of life. But true prayer is far more than a spare tire to be used in times of need. It is not a last resort when conditions are desperate.

Prayer holds many advantages for people who make it part of their daily routine. To wait patiently in the presence of God creates an opportunity to experience the Holy Spirit.

When your prayer life is consistent, life takes on a whole new meaning. Rushing headlong into things gives way to calm and balanced judgment. You start to do things according to God's way. The patterns of your life begin to unfold. It is breathtaking how God guides those who turn to Him in prayer and obey what He says.

God talks to you through prayer. The person who prays will be enlightened and find guidance. Prayer confirms the presence of God in your heart and opens a new experience of life and wisdom.

Jesus, Savior, Your burden is light and Your yoke is easy. Help me to take up my cross and follow You.

~ Amen ~

Prepare yourself for life through prayer

Pray continually. (1 Thes. 5:17)

The future is the great unknown. But you can prepare for it. The most effective way of doing this is by developing a healthy prayer life. It will provide you with strength in moments of weakness and comfort in times of sorrow.

Many people will tell you that praying is a natural instinct. This may be true, but an effective prayer life is the result of a disciplined and sensitive attitude before God. If you are sincere, you will not only pray when you feel like it, but you will rejoice in the privilege and share each fleeting emotion and feeling with your Master.

Share your joy in prayer with God while the sun shines, and there will be no feeling of panic when the storm comes up. You will merely share in the quiet conviction that God is in full control and that you have prepared adequately for every situation in life through prayer. God will do the rest!

How wonderful, heavenly Father, to praise and to glorify You. I want to sing the praises of Your great love and faithfulness for all nations to hear.

~ Amen ~

MARCH 17

Let your prayer life flourish

But grow in the grace and knowledge of our Lord and Savior Jesus Christ. (2 Pet. 3:18)

Prayer is so easy! Prayer is so difficult! If you have tried nurturing a meaningful prayer life, you will know that both these statements are true. With good intentions you put aside time to spend in the presence of God, but as soon as you settle down, something shatters your privacy. The telephone rings, someone knocks at the door, or you remember something you forgot to do. Satan uses all kinds of ploys to keep you from praying.

It might help to make these disturbances part of your prayers. Take the obstacles that Satan places in your way and turn them into objects of prayer. Then you will thwart Satan and his evil plans.

Prayer is not static, but a living, pulsating power that should constantly draw you closer to your heavenly Father. If your prayer life is weak and ineffective, or if you have stopped praying altogether, you are like a car battery that has not functioned for a long time.

Regularly recharge your devotional batteries through prayer. And then your prayer life will flourish and bless your whole life.

Without You, Lord, I cannot do anything. Fill me with Your Spirit so that I can hold onto You.
~ Amen ~

When God is far off

"My God, my God, why have you forsaken me? Why are you so far from saving me?" (Ps. 22:1)

We all go through periods of darkness and doubt on our spiritual journeys. Our spiritual life becomes dry and so we derive no inspiration from prayer or meditation.

These times of spiritual drought could be regarded as training schools for prayer. Without times in the dark valleys we cannot appreciate the mountain tops. It is the struggle to rise above the depths of depression that generates spiritual strength and stamina for the battles of life.

If you want to grow into maturity, then the valley experience is imperative. It is very easy to allow your vision of God to grow dim and to forget His earlier love and assistance. But God's love for you never changes, regardless of how you feel.

Times spent in the spiritual valley can be beneficial, if you remember that you will not stay there forever. You are simply passing through.

If God feels distant, and you are deeply aware of your own shortcomings, then stop for a while and assure yourself in prayer that He is with you. The darkness will gradually be transformed into light.

Thank You Lord, that You are always close to me even when I go through the dark valleys.

~ Amen ~

MARCH 19

Don't bargain with God

Do not test the LORD your God as you did at Massah.
(Deut. 6:16)

You cannot bargain with God. There are people – some quite innocently – who, in their prayers, offer God something in exchange for the fulfillment of their requests.

It is vital that you realize that everything you are and everything you have comes only through the grace of God. Because He loves you He provides in all your needs according to the riches of His grace. It is also essential that you accept that you belong to Him. You have been redeemed through the sacrifice of Jesus Christ on the cross, and now you belong to Him. This is why you cannot bargain with Him, offering Him something in exchange for the answer you seek.

The right approach to prayer is to lay all your concerns and requests before Him and then to wait faithfully. Accept that whatever He ordains for you will be good, and acknowledge it as being within the will of the Father.

If this is your attitude in your prayers, you will experience the peace of God that flows from faith in and acceptance of the will of your heavenly Father.

Your will for me, O Father, is only good. Therefore I will wait patiently for Your answer to every prayer that I bring before You.

~ Amen ~

It is perfectly natural to pray

He will respond to the prayer of the destitute; he will not despise their plea. (Ps. 102:17)

Most Christians wish they could spend more time in prayer. They realize the inadequacy of their prayer life, but when they do try to pray with depth and meaning, they are hindered by wandering thoughts and a restless spirit.

Prayer is something completely natural, even though some people think otherwise. Prayer is the heartbeat of the soul. You may understand nothing of schools of prayer or methods of contemplation, but every time you think of God there is something deep inside you that yearns for a Reality that you cannot always explain. This hunger of your soul and your seeking thoughts are a form of prayer.

While prescribed prayers and orthodox methods of praying may help you to enter into the presence of God, it is the cry of the troubled heart, so often expressed in confusion and despair, that moves the loving heart of God. Every time you think of Him, you are busy praying. Therefore do not feel discouraged if your prayer life seems inadequate. Every thought that is directed at God is a prayer that connects you to Him.

O Hearer of prayers, I praise and thank You for prayer that carries me into Your holy presence.

~ Amen ~

The essence of true prayer

During the days of Jesus' life on earth, he offered up prayers and petitions with loud cries and tears to the one who could save him from death, and he was heard because of his reverent submission. (Heb. 5:7)

It is a great tragedy that so many people regard prayer so casually. For some it has degenerated into a meaningless ritual; and others use it as a panic button in a time of crisis.

While there is not the slightest doubt that God hears the call of a distressed heart and He is always ready to answer, we must be willing to spend quality time in prayer. If prayer becomes a top priority for you, it will also bring about satisfaction and fulfillment in your life.

Prayer does not only consist of directing your words to God. You need to make time to become still before God and to wait on Him. You must be sensitive to the moving of the Holy Spirit and to His guidance. Prayer is always a two-way interaction: your conversation with God, and your believing, listening to and obeying what God is saying.

Surrender yourself completely to God. Lay your desires, and those people whom you pray for before Him and then pray that His will, not yours, be done. In the same way that the living Christ discovered and obeyed the will of God, you must do so too.

Lord, You who hear our prayers, enable me to be still in Your presence and to hear what You say to me.

~ Amen ~

Precious moments

The LORD is good to those whose hope is in him, to the one who seeks him; it is good to wait quietly for the salvation of the LORD. (Lam. 3:25-26)

When life gets too busy, we need to pause quietly so that we can reestablish our values and put things in the right perspective. It sounds foolish to speak about stopping everything when you are at your busiest. But it is more foolish to think that you can succeed without quiet times with God.

Our Lord, when He was on earth, needed to withdraw to spend time with His Father. How can we then think that we do not need times of refreshing that come from spending time quietly with God?

Make time to meet with God. Such a time is like an oasis where your strength is replenished, and a time of refreshment and spiritual growth.

If you do this conscientiously, you will return to your busy life with a feeling of balance and tranquility of mind and the powerful assurance that God is with you and that He grants you His wisdom, love and grace.

Loving Father, thank You for those precious moments when I am so aware of Your presence that joy overwhelms me.

~ Amen ~

MARCH 23

Prayer behind closed doors

But when you pray, go into your room, close the door and pray to your Father, who is unseen. Then your Father, who sees what is done in secret, will reward you. (Mt. 6:6)

It is an extremely difficult discipline to wait on God. It is far easier to talk to God than to listen to Him in silence. Wandering and annoying thoughts, bitterness in your heart, false pride that harbors unforgiveness toward someone, and many other confusing and destructive thoughts hijack the precious time that you want to spend in God's presence.

Your thoughts do not exist in a vacuum. Therefore you have the responsibility to select your thoughts with care. In the time that you put aside to be alone with God, your thoughts should be completely focused on Him. That is why the Master commands us to isolate ourselves behind closed doors in God's presence.

In isolation you are then completely focused on the Father and you can dialog with Him. Find a private place where you will not be disturbed when you go to pray. Then wait on Him and listen to what He says through His Holy Spirit.

Never underestimate the value of private and intimate time with God.

Eternal Rock, in You alone I trust, because You will help me. Your kindness and love are abundant.

~ Amen ~

Prayer leads to action

So what shall I do? I will pray with my spirit, but I will also pray with my mind; I will sing with my spirit, but I will also sing with my mind. (1 Cor. 14:15)

At times we beg God to answer our prayers when we actually need to take action ourselves. Often, instead of pleading with God to supply a special need, we should be doing something about it. If you are lonely and keep asking God for a meaningful friendship, you need to start by offering your friendship to others. Do you constantly ask God to save you from debt – and yet you refuse to control your spending or stick to a budget?

Answer to prayer is often found in a balanced approach to life. If you handle problems prayerfully, you will develop divinely inspired common sense. If you are filled with the Holy Spirit, He will guide you and give you the ability to act in accordance with His will and purpose for your life.

Prayer requires that we cooperate with God to bring about the answers to our requests. We are responsible to develop our potential. Prayer enables Christ's followers to tackle life with courage. It gives you the assurance that God's guidance and wisdom are always available for those who receive them with a sensitive heart and an open mind.

Living Savior, I thank and praise You that I have been called to be Your partner in prayer.

~ Amen ~

MARCH 25

It's never too late to pray

I lie awake; I have become like a bird alone on a roof. (Ps. 102:7)

Many people rob themselves of experiencing peace with God because they feel unworthy. When they are in great need, they don't draw close to God because they have not spent much time with Him in the past. And in times of crisis they then feel it is not right to come to Him. Others are burdened with feelings of guilt or shame and feel that they cannot approach God.

Jesus Christ promised that He will not cast out anyone who comes to Him. He did not come to seek those who are righteous, but to call sinners to repentance.

Throughout Scripture you will read about God's unfathomable love and compassion towards all people – the good and the bad; those who deserved it and those who didn't.

It is never too late for you to turn to the Christ who forgives, and to pour out your needs before Him. The murderer on the cross did that in his dying moments and he received redemption. Christ will hear your cry of despair and will surround you with His love.

Holy God, I sincerely thank You, that with You, it's never too late to ask for forgiveness, and that You stand ready to answer my every prayer.

~ Amen ~

When you pray

One of them ... came back, praising God in a loud voice.
(Lk. 17:15)

A large percentage of our prayers consist of requests. We are always asking things of God: we pray for healing, for guidance, for deliverance from our distress, for peace and for God to provide in our needs. We seek God's help in matters pertaining to the church as well as the state. Analyze your own prayers and you may find that this is true of you too.

There is nothing wrong with this, because our Lord Himself invited us to come to Him with our needs. However, what is our response when God answers our prayers? How do we react when He, in His infinite wisdom, does not give us what we ask for? Or when He gives us something different from what we asked?

When you present your prayers to the Lord, leave them to Him and His will. Be grateful that He hears and understands you. Know that in His own perfect time and in His own unique way He will answer in the way that is best for you. Gratefully accept everything that God bestows upon you from His treasure house and be content with His will.

I praise and thank You, O God, for all the gifts of grace that I receive undeservedly from Your hand. Even when You say no to me, I know that it is for my own good.

~ Amen ~

MARCH 27

In the service of God

Do your best to present yourself to God as one approved, a workman who does not need to be ashamed and who correctly handles the word of truth. (2 Tim. 2:15)

God has many workers who are active in His service. They attend church meetings, do many good deeds, and seldom have free time on their hands. This can have bleak consequences. You can become so involved in God's work that you lose sight of what God wants you to do. Then you are diligently working for God without working with Him. You may even delude yourself into thinking that you are doing extremely important work.

But then one day, when it is almost too late, something just withers in your soul; you become tense, and you simply snap. You cease all your Christian activities because of a nervous breakdown, and a life that may have been of great importance to God is lost.

The most important duty of any Christian worker is to maintain and strengthen a relationship with God every day. If you are too busy to spend time with Him in daily prayer, you are simply too busy to be an effective servant for Him.

Loving Master, I humbly ask that You will inspire and strengthen me for the service that I offer to You in gratitude for my redemption.
~ Amen ~

Prayer: the challenge

And being in anguish, he prayed more earnestly. (Lk. 22:44)

Contrary to popular belief, prayer is not always an exciting experience. Of course there are uplifting moments when God becomes a glorious reality to you and you experience intimate union with Him. Then there is a joy in prayer that is not easy to explain in words. If, however, this is the only aspect of prayer that you have experienced, then you have been missing the depth and variety of true prayer.

You will experience the full impact of the challenge of prayer when you ask God to bring about spiritual maturity in you, and when you ask Him to use you in His service. You will soon discover that your prayers extend to involve other people as well. Through your prayers you bring God into contact with those who are in need: perhaps a child who went astray; a hungry, lonely person; or someone who is suffering.

As God lays the needs of people on your heart, you begin to understand the great responsibility of prayer. Sharing in this privilege enables you to live in love towards God and your fellowmen.

Today I want to pray for the strength to intercede for others and for the ability to be used in Your service.

~ Amen ~

What is the focus of your prayers?

MARCH 29

"Since you have asked for this and not for long life or wealth for yourself, nor have asked for the death of your enemies but for discernment in administering justice, I will do what you have asked." (1 Kgs. 3:11-12)

There is a strong temptation to focus on "self" in prayer. Many people only go before God with lists of requests. The danger of this is that your prayers become self-centered and that the praise and gratitude to God, as well as the needs of others, take a back seat. This leads to disillusionment, because, if you do not get the answers you want, you could end up distancing yourself from God.

Every prayer that you pray must echo the immortal words of Christ: *"Yet not as I will, but as you will"* (Mt. 26:39). This is the highest practice in faith: complete surrender of your prayers to the Lord, while you yield to His will and commit yourself to Him. In this way you acknowledge His sovereignty over your life and all your circumstances.

When you succeed in committing your prayers completely to God, while trusting Him absolutely with your welfare and future, an indescribable feeling of peace will descend on your life. You will come to the realization that Christ has His hand on you and that the Holy Spirit has guided you onto the perfect path.

Lord, You guide me when words fail me in prayer. Your mercy intervenes and gives me peace.

~ Amen ~

Surrender your prayer life to God

"Lord, teach us to pray." (Lk. 11:1)

Most Christians are very aware of their own inability to pray according to the will of God. They realize that they should pray more regularly and so ask the Lord to make their prayer life more meaningful. But they forget that an effective prayer life depends partly on themselves.

Christ sacrificed Himself for all who embrace Him in faith and trust Him as their Savior and Redeemer. He gave Himself freely, but He will enrich your life only as far as you will allow Him to. The depth and quality of your devotion to Him will be reflected in the strength of your prayer life.

If you surrender yourself more completely to Christ, you will be increasingly aware of His living presence in your life. You will discover channels of communication with Him that you can use anywhere at any time. If this happens, your prayers will become the motivating force of your everyday life. It does not mean a thing to ask God for a meaningful and positive prayer life unless you do your share to develop it.

Lord, teach me not to fret about what tomorrow may bring. Teach me to quietly trust in You, because You are good and all-wise.

~ Amen ~

MARCH

Be fervent and persevere in prayer

So he left them and went away once more and prayed the third time, saying the same thing. (Mt. 26:44)

31 There are many committed Christians who experience problems with their prayer life. They wonder why, if God is all-seeing and omniscient, they need to persevere in the discipline of prayer. They feel guilty about "troubling" God over and over with issues that He is already aware of.

Remember that you often know about problems in people's lives but that you do not usually intervene until asked to do so. If you feel that a particular matter in your life needs God's intervention, do not hesitate to bring it before Him. Remind Him of His promises and ask Him to take care of the situation.

If you feel that something is worth praying for, it deserves more than just a passing mention before God. Present your requests before Him with sincerity and fervor. God will never tire of listening to you if you come to Him in the Name of Christ.

The Holy Spirit teaches you fervor and perseverance, and therefore you should learn to be sensitive to God's voice through the Holy Spirit.

In distress I call to You, O Lord, because only You can grant me peace. Thank You for hearing my prayers and for always answering my cry for help.

~ Amen ~

April

Holy is Your being, O God,
more pure than the light of the sun!
Holy Father, by grace You call me,
a sinful man, to a life of holiness.
Without Your abundant grace
I would not even be able to start out
on the path of sanctification.
But, through my Savior, Jesus, Your Son,
the possibilities of living a holy life are unlimited.
Holy Spirit, flow through me
and cleanse me from all my sin.
Capture my thoughts and submit them to Your will.
Touch my words with Your godly grace.
May every deed I do be done in love
and may I reflect the holiness of my Lord.
I give You all the honor and praise.
You are the light of my life
and the guide along my path.
You are my Savior O Lord,
and the King of my heart!

~ Amen ~

The ultimate purpose of life

For we who are alive are always being given over to death for Jesus' sake, so that his life may be revealed in our mortal body. (2 Cor. 4:11)

Many people seem to have ulterior motives for leading a good life. There are also many people whose dedicated service to their fellowmen is inspired by their commitment to Jesus Christ and humanity is enriched by them.

True Christian service can only be the expression of an honest and sincere relationship with Jesus Christ. As a Christian you are not only called to do good works, but also to reflect the life of Christ in your thoughts and deeds.

The fact that we are called to be Christlike, offers a challenge that many people try to evade. Yet this wonderful fellowship and intimacy are the Lord's gifts to those who love Him and have committed their lives to Him.

If Christlikeness is the goal of your life, it will give you a much better understanding of the needs and sorrows of your fellowmen. The closer you live to Christ, the deeper your compassion will be for those with whom you live and work.

Savior and Lord, may Your beauty be reflected in my life, in my thoughts, words and deeds today.

~ Amen ~

The power of the Holy Spirit

APRIL 2

Live by the Spirit, and you will not gratify the desires of the sinful nature. (Gal. 5:16)

Much has been written and spoken about the importance of placing Christ first in your life. The call to surrender to His will and to obey His commands is often emphasized and Christians are encouraged to turn away from the world in order to follow Christ.

Many sincere believers try to meet these expectations in their efforts to lead a life that conforms to Christ's. But it is much easier said than done.

Because of the many temptations and diversions that we face in daily life, it is very difficult to live a life that meets all Jesus' standards. It requires an extremely strong will and character, which is far beyond the ability of ordinary people. The pace and pressure of modern life puts us under enormous stress.

It is under these circumstances that you must open your life to the influence of the Holy Spirit. Invite Him to take control of your entire being, and then you will experience the power of Jesus Christ, which enables you to overcome every stumbling block as you live in and for Him.

Come, O Holy Spirit, and fill my life. Then I will live boldly and be strong in my convictions.

~ Amen ~

Renew your character

Therefore, if anyone is in Christ, he is a new creation; the old has gone, the new has come! (2 Cor. 5:17)

Other people observe our characters and they base their impressions of us on what they see. Only a few people take the trouble to develop an agreeable character. Many people put on a plastic smile and put up a pleasant front for special occasions. But when the moment has past, they slip back into their old patterns.

Many people believe that a character cannot be changed. This is not true. If this were so, the redeeming love of Christ would have been in vain. Sinners can change into saints and unpleasant people can become amiable when the love of Christ enters their hearts.

When you open your life to the Spirit of the living Christ, and His influence is reflected in your life, a transfiguration takes place in your character and lifestyle. Your calling as a Christian is not merely to be a "good person" – although, obviously that is what you will be. You will also be totally surrendered to your Lord and that will change your character.

Your love is always with me. Father, draw me closer into Your circle of love every day. I want to remain in You.

~ Amen ~

Christlikeness

APRIL 4

Dear friends, now we are children of God, and what we will be has not yet been made known. But we know that when he appears, we shall be like him, for we shall see him as he is. (1 Jn. 3:2)

It should be the goal of every Christian to mold his life according to the example set by Jesus Christ. This will vary according to every person's nature and personality, but the desire will always be to grow into the likeness of the Master.

The unconditional acceptance of the lordship of Christ is the beginning of a new and satisfying way of life. Because you now belong to Him, all your energy should be aimed at becoming like Him. He becomes your role model and your goal.

Obviously it is impossible to achieve this in your own strength. When you accepted Jesus as the Lord of your life, He came to live in your heart. If you ask Him, He will give you His Holy Spirit. Then your faith will come alive and you will be able to live your whole life in obedience to Him.

In this way you will begin to develop a Christlike character.

Lord, I ask that Your Spirit would fill me and enable me to be more like You today.

~ Amen ~

Your calling to be Christlike

"On that day you will realize that I am in my Father, and you are in me, and I am in you." (Jn. 14:20)

The life and teachings of Jesus Christ pose the greatest challenge that anyone could ever face. Many people who acknowledge Him as the perfect example try to follow Him by committing themselves to do good works. They make great sacrifices in the hope that this will help them to become like Him.

While all disciples should have a sincere desire to be like Jesus, all the effort in the world will not help them to achieve this goal. Becoming like Christ begins in the heart and mind. The presence of the Living Christ is found in our hearts and we can draw strength from Him to grow spiritually and in beauty and truth.

Unless the presence of Christ is a living reality in your heart, it will be impossible to reflect His personality in your life.

The challenge and call to be more Christlike is an intensely personal one. It is a challenge to a deeper and more intimate relationship with the Lord, in which you allow Him to reveal Himself through your life.

Holy Master, through Your great grace and abiding presence I grow every day to become more like You.

~ Amen ~

True spirituality

APRIL 6

"You are the light of the world. Let your light so shine before men, that they may see your good works and glorify your Father in heaven." (Mt. 5:14, 16)

In many circles of society the word "spirituality" is not very popular. It conjures images of well-meaning people who are intensely religious, but don't succeed in handling the practical problems of everyday life.

True spirituality is the most beautiful and powerful force known to mankind. It is free from all deception and false piety and is able to handle any situation that arises. This is because true spirituality is the expression of inner peace that is the direct result of ongoing fellowship with the Lord.

The truly spiritual person is essentially practical. An employee who is truly spiritual will reveal his spirituality through excellent and honest work and service. Regardless of the role you have in life, you will fulfill it to the glory of God if you develop true spirituality.

The rich fruit of a truly sprritual life is there for everyone to see. This is the essence of true spirituality: to love Christ with all your soul and mind and to allow His love to flow through you.

Loving Master, through Your Spirit, let Your great and wonderful love flow through me.

~ Amen ~

A good reputation

They loved praise from men more than praise from God.
(Jn. 12:43)

Your good reputation is of inestimable worth. It cannot be gained overnight, nor can it be bought by favors given with ulterior motives. It can only be gained by living a noble life.

Standards that are founded on essential values ought not to be influenced by the opinions of other people. Your standards should not be those of the world, but those of God. If you allow your reputation to be shaped by other people's opinions and expectations of you, your life will be governed by vacillating values.

When you live to please God alone, you accept principles that create a strong character and a good reputation. Your word becomes your bond; your candor is tempered with love; honesty becomes an integral part of your being; and, because you are aware of your own vulnerability, you refrain from harsh criticism. Living to please God has a powerful influence on your life. If you honor God and allow Him to govern your life, you will have the respect of those who live according to God's standards.

Holy Lord Jesus, help me to live to please You alone. May Your values always be manifested in my life.

~ Amen ~

APRIL 8

The decisive test of discipleship

"By this all men will know that you are my disciples, if you love one another." (Jn. 13:35)

The Christian's standards are those of Christ and, in our conduct and attitude, we need to strive to reflect the image of Christ. Christian discipleship demands an honorable way of life and the doing of good deeds. It is impossible to live in intimacy with Christ without something of His loveliness being reflected in our lives. Because you are a Christian, your life should differ in many ways from that of non-Christians. Not only does the Lord expect this, but the world expects it of you as well.

The litmus test of true Christlikeness is the love Christians have for one another. Good deeds without love lack the incisive power of godly discipleship, and faith becomes a series of good deeds that lack inspiration and purpose.

If we find it difficult to love, we need only open our lives to His Spirit, and allow Him to love others through us. It is the true love of Christ that flows through us that will demonstrate to all that we are His disciples.

I ask that Your love will take possession of my life, O Lord, so that I will reflect the quality of Your love.

~ Amen ~

The fruit of the Spirit

But the fruit of the Spirit is love, joy, peace, patience, kindness, goodness, faithfulness, gentleness, self-control. (Gal. 5:22)

Christians should have a constant desire to become more and more like the Lord in their thoughts and actions. For every serious follower of the living Christ, the challenge to become more and more conformed to His image cannot be deferred.

The fruit of the Spirit are aspects of the character of Christ. They have been called the nine main signs of God's presence, and every disciple who yields to Christ can possess these qualities. With Christ's help we can achieve this. That which is impossible for you, becomes possible through Him.

Take each one of the fruits and meditate on them in your quiet times until they become an integral part of your nature. Consider what it means to say, "In Christ I am filled with love," until you feel His love fill your life. This may sound like a time-consuming process, but in matters that concern the spiritual life, growth cannot be hastened. Then you will develop a well-balanced spiritual life that will be to Christ's honor and glory.

Mighty God, I desire to have the full fruit of the Holy Spirit manifest in my life.

~ Amen ~

APRIL 10

Faith and good deeds

"Therefore we conclude that a man is justified by faith apart from the deeds of the law." (Rom. 3:28)

Good works are the by-product of a Christian lifestyle. It is impossible to live with an awareness of the presence of Christ and still do mean or evil deeds.

Many committed Christians believe that by performing noble deeds they obtain a good standing that will eventually get them into heaven. We must remember, however, that many agnostics and atheists are "good" people who fight for the rights of those who are less privileged.

The difference between a Christian and a "good" person is that the latter is good because he tries to be good. The Christian lives in a vital relationship with the living Christ and is good because the life of His Lord is reflected in him. This incurs an attitude of inner peace and joy in a life through which God is glorified and His will performed.

A life that is inspired by the Holy Spirit has a quality that will rise above natural goodness and will make something of Jesus Christ visible in our lives.

Lord Jesus, I ask that You would show me what needs to be done so that I can show others the greatness of Your grace and love.

~ Amen ~

What do we owe one another?

April 11

Bear with each other and forgive whatever grievances you may have ... Forgive as the Lord forgave you. And over all these virtues put on love, which binds them all together. (Col. 3:13-14)

If Christ lives in you, you will be kind and patient toward your fellowman. Courtesy is about taking others and their feelings into consideration.

A person who is truly courteous is humble and never tries to impress others. His attitude is the same whether he is talking to his equals or his subordinates. He treats everyone alike, regardless of race, color or religious creed. He rejoices in making his neighbor's path easier to travel. This attitude comes from regular contact with God.

It is impossible to love and serve God while at the same time treating your neighbor with contempt and disrespect. If you treat only certain people with respect you expose the superficiality of your spiritual experience. Courtesy is not something that you can switch on and off. It is either something that comes from your heart, or an act of hypocrisy that fools no one.

When the Holy Spirit lives in you, you reflect the qualities of Christ in your life. Love and courtesy are the basic characteristics of the Christian life, and good manners are the product of true Christianity.

Favor me, Lord Jesus, with the gift of courtesy that springs from a heart that is in harmony with You.

~ Amen ~

APRIL 12

Can people see Jesus in you?

If Timothy comes, see to it that he has nothing to fear while he is with you, for he is carrying on the work of the Lord. (1 Cor. 16:10)

So many problems originate from the inability to communicate. Interpersonal relationships are of the utmost importance for our social well-being, and yet sadly we often pay little attention to this important aspect of life.

Jesus commanded us to love one another, and so Christian love may be basically defined as doing good and doing so in a pleasant way. It necessarily follows that when we do something for someone else the love of Jesus should be evident. Treating someone with contempt directly conflicts with everything that the Master taught and did, and everything that He expects of you and me.

In order to establish good relationships among people it is essential to follow Jesus' example. Seek the help of the Holy Spirit and ask Him to take control of your life so that you can act with love, peace, joy, patience, kindness, compassion, faithfulness, tolerance and self-control. This will be your contribution to making the world a better place.

Holy Spirit, please help me to act towards all people with the love that Jesus showed.

~ Amen ~

Inner beauty

May the favor of the Lord our God rest upon us; establish the work of our hands for us – yes, establish the work of our hands. (Ps. 90:17)

People sometimes spend large amounts of money trying to make themselves beautiful. Others take courses to develop their characters and social skills. To be well-groomed and skilled in the social etiquette of high society doesn't create a strong character or inner beauty. The true beauty of a person's life has its basis in inner character. We can create an illusion of outward beauty, but if a person's heart is self-centered and malicious, it will be a hard and unattractive beauty.

Others may not be physically beautiful, but have an inner life which is so beautiful that people notice only the inner beauty that radiates from them.

The inner life can only prosper and be reflected in outward beauty when there is perfect harmony between us and our Creator.

True beauty does not start at the cosmetics counter, but in the sacred place of intimacy where you spend time alone with God. That is where you gather inner peace of mind and dignity that keeps you balanced at all times. Allow the beauty of your spirit to develop through your fellowship with God and then your whole life will be beautiful.

Lord, I pray that my life will at all times reflect Your beauty and so draw people to You.

~ Amen ~

APRIL

It all depends upon you

In the same way, faith by itself, if it is not accompanied by action, is dead. (Jas. 2:17)

14 Being a Christian means that you accept responsibility for your own life. You may reason that God is in control and therefore everything is His responsibility. But if God is to accomplish anything with your life, He must have your full cooperation.

God has given you an intellect so that you can learn about Him and His Word and then apply that knowledge to your life. Obedience to Him will lead to a positive attitude to life, a life lived in harmony with His will.

People work hard in their pursuit of happiness. Many people ask God to make them happy, but they hold on to negative thought patterns and a disgruntled attitude toward life.

A self-centered life, where your own interests take precedence over the needs of others, ignores the Scriptural truth that reaching out to others brings happiness to ourselves. You cannot be truly happy unless you help those in need around you.

Help me to set an example to others. Lend me a helping hand so that my conduct will always carry the seal of love.

~ *Amen* ~

The joy of life in Christ

"Blessed rather are those who hear the word of God and obey it." (Lk. 11:28)

Many people's attitude toward keeping Christian principles is one of reluctant submission to a tiresome yet necessary discipline. Tiresome because it limits or suppresses our pleasure, but necessary for the well-being of the soul.

This should never be the attitude of the Christian believer, because Jesus came precisely so that you can have life in all its abundance. He wants you to have a life of purpose, vigor and joy. The entire Christian experience centers on a caring heavenly Father who desires only the best for His children. His love is so incomprehensibly great that He sacrificed His Son for you. Jesus offers you forgiveness, redemption and the promise of eternal life. Through His Holy Spirit He enables you to live in faith, confidence and victory.

What more could anyone ask of life? Here you have the promise of the very best that life can offer and all that God expects of you is to accept His sovereignty in your life. Surely this is little enough to ask in exchange for a life of fulfillment and joy?

Lord Jesus, I rejoice in the knowledge that You redeemed me and granted me a life of joy and fulfillment. My heart sings in praise and gratitude.

~ Amen ~

APRIL 16

Be productive

The Lord said to Satan, "Where have you come from?" Satan answered the Lord, "From roaming through the earth and going back and forth in it." (Job 1:7)

There are many people who are constantly on the go and yet seem to achieve little. They seldom have time to become still and consider the beauty and love of God. They live at such a frantic pace that they have no time for any of the ordinary small pleasures of life. Their lives are busy but unproductive.

To live a productive life it is essential to plan wisely. Without a sense of direction your life will become meaningless and frustrating.

How is it possible to plan your life properly? Young people will have different goals from those who are older, but in all cases careful planning is required. It is God who guides us. To understand and execute God's plan for your life requires faith, patience and courage. Faith to believe that God has a plan for your life; patience to wait while He unfolds His plan to you; courage to obey His commands.

If you carry out God's will in your life, you will be constructively busy, and as you cooperate with God, you will get to know Him even more intimately.

Heavenly Father, when I am busy, may it be to carry out Your holy will for my life.

~ Amen ~

In partnership with God

"Now let the fear of the LORD be upon you. Judge carefully, for with the LORD our God there is no injustice or partiality or bribery." (2 Chr. 19:7)

APRIL 17

There are people who think that religion and business should be kept separate. Some people feel that the two areas simply do not mix, while others become uncomfortable when they consider their business practices in the light of Christian principles.

God very definitely has a place in your business and social life, just as He does in your spiritual life, and you cannot eliminate Him from one of these spheres without harming yourself. Your entire life should be governed by Christian principles and you should bear witness to your Christianity, regardless of the sphere of life that you are moving in.

The surest way to reflect integrity in all your interactions is to make the living Christ your business partner. Whatever you do, scrutinize it through the eyes of Jesus; ask yourself how He would have reacted and what He would have done in your circumstances.

Follow Christ's example and you will be assured of a virtuous life that will earn you the respect of everyone you interact with.

Lord Jesus, I am not ashamed to acknowledge You as Lord of my life, or to profess Your name under any circumstances.

~ Amen ~

APRIL 18

The right way

"Walk in all the way that the LORD your God has commanded you, so that you may live and prosper and prolong your days in the land that you will possess." (Deut. 5:33)

Many people maintain high standards of honesty, integrity and righteousness, yet they see others prospering in spite of their questionable lives. When this happens, the danger is that they will be tempted to compromise and follow deceitful principles.

If you should be tempted in this way, then remember that you can never hide your actions from God. He knows your life inside out and His light shines into every dark and hidden corner. Your conscience will be quick to address the issue and make you feel uncomfortable. You will feel ill at ease and unhappy because you know what you are doing is wrong in His sight.

To ensure a life of peace and liberty for yourself you must follow the example of Jesus Christ. His whole life was a testimony of honesty, integrity, righteousness, compassion and love. Then you will experience the abundant life He promises you. And you will taste the joy and fulfillment that are the portion of those who walk along the way of Truth.

Holy Spirit, Your way is far above my ways. Help me to follow You and obey You in all things.

~ Amen ~

God's way

Good and upright is the Lord; therefore he instructs sinners in his ways. (Ps. 25:8)

The pressure exerted by the sinful world is felt by young and old; temptations are many and are offered on a silver platter; the variety of detours make it extremely difficult to follow the right path. The constant questioning of standards and morality presents a fundamental danger that our principles may be compromised.

There is only one way to live your life and that is to follow God's ways. In His commandments, He set out the basic rules for a holy and devout life. Christ became a living example, demonstrating to us how life should be lived.

Even though centuries have passed, nothing has changed with regard to the way of life that is acceptable and pleasing to God. Christ is still the way, the truth and the life, and the path of righteousness is still that of obedience to God in all things.

If you open your heart and life to the indwelling Holy Spirit, you will become increasingly aware of His influence. Follow His guidance and you will know that the path you are on is the way God wants you to go.

Search me, O God, and know my heart; test me and know my anxious thoughts. See if there is any offensive way in me, and lead me in the way everlasting (Ps. 139:23-24).

~ Amen ~

APRIL

Live in fellowship with Christ

God, who has called you into fellowship with his Son Jesus Christ our Lord, is faithful. (1 Cor. 1:9)

20 To share in the life of Jesus Christ implies unlimited possibilities, but also great responsibilities. Your understanding of God is deepened, your vision of what your life can be is expanded and you become aware of the abiding presence of Christ. But such intimacy with the Lord carries certain responsibilities. The characteristics of God must be reflected in your life through love, honesty, unselfishness and integrity.

To reflect the Spirit of Christ to the best of your ability you should develop a vision of what you can achieve for the Lord. You are no longer restricted by deep-seated fears and doubts, but can move confidently forward in the strength of the living Christ.

Christ offers Himself to you so that you can share in His life and share your life with Him. But this offer only becomes a reality when you accept it in faith. You may have the knowledge of this glorious truth, but until you have made it your own you will not experience the strength and joy of the presence of Jesus Christ in your life.

Lord Jesus, I invite You anew to come into my life and to do Your work on earth through me. I now open my heart and life to You.

~ Amen ~

True holiness

"For my thoughts are not your thoughts, neither are your ways my ways" says the Lord. (Is. 55:8)

Many people believe that living a holy life causes you to miss out on the good things in life. It seems incomprehensible that a life of fullness and great joy could be linked to holiness. Yet true holiness is the most dynamic, creative and meaningful lifestyle in the world.

To be holy implies that you live in right relationship with God. It causes you to enjoy life to the full and also gives you a greater understanding of people.

True holiness consists of the burning desire to become more like Christ and a willingness to reach out to people. Thus the image of Christ is reflected by you in the community where you live.

The secret of a balanced and rewarding life is to live in such a way that it is easy for the Lord to reveal Himself through you. This is the way of true sanctification, but it is also the road to a successful life according to God's standard.

Teach me, O Holy Spirit, the true meaning of holiness and enable me to live a life that will bring glory and honor to God each day.

~ Amen ~

APRIL 22

Be honest

He who conceals his sins does not prosper, but whoever confesses and renounces them finds mercy. (Prov. 28:13)

The well-known proverb: "Honesty is the best policy" contains an irrevocable truth. But there are many people who find it difficult to live by. Some ignore it on purpose, while others, caught in a web of doubt and fear, find themselves unable to handle the consequences of honesty. Then they try to conceal their shortcomings or failures. In the process they sink deeper into new problems until it eventually seems impossible to disentangle themselves.

Such behavior inevitably leads to mental anguish and stress, because our emotions and nervous system cannot cope with the negative influences caused by deception.

We all make mistakes of one sort or another. Christ, who lived among flawed people, is aware of and sympathetic to human fallibility. If you did something wrong, don't try and hide it with a lie. Trust in the love, forgiveness and courage that Jesus offers you. Acknowledge and confess your error and try to correct it. This is the only way you will find peace for your soul.

Thank You, Holy Spirit of God, that You taught me that I may live in peace by being honest at all times.

~ Amen ~

Grow through humility towards confidence

APRIL 23

Rather think of yourself with sober judgment, in accordance with the measure of faith God has given you. (Rom. 12:3)

In the eyes of God you are of immeasurable value. God does not create nobodies. It is your privilege and duty to develop your character and personality to its fullest potential.

How is it possible to be set free from inferiority?

When you realize that Jesus Christ lives in you, you will be renewed and come to an understanding of what life is really about. You will no longer retreat from daily challenges, because you will know that the strength you possess is not of your own making, but comes from the Spirit of Christ that works in you.

Through humility you will grow towards God-centered self-confidence.

Thank You, my Savior and Friend, that I may rejoice: I can do everything through Him who gives me strength. I want to sing Your praise and my thanks!

~ Amen ~

Remember who you are!

APRIL 24

So God created man in his own image, in the image of God he created him. (Gen. 1:27)

When it seems as if nothing in your life is working out, when loneliness takes hold of you and despondency descends upon you, it is time to remember a few spiritual facts.

You were created in the image of God. Yes, this image *has* been damaged and perhaps you *have* forgotten your rich spiritual heritage. But the fact remains that you are a spiritual being. Knowing this should flood you with new hope and inspiration. You do not need to be at the whim of moods beyond your control. You have been created for spiritual greatness, and when you live in the awareness of His presence, you will be fulfilled.

If your life is hindered by the stress and tension created by feelings of inadequacy, you will find freedom in drawing on the abundance of God's strength. This will enable you to face life confidently, assured that His Spirit is working in you.

My Savior, Jesus Christ, because of my spiritual heritage and the awareness of Your living presence I can meet life with confidence.

~ Amen ~

Live one day at a time

For today the L<small>ORD</small> will appear to you. (Lev. 9:4)

We all become impatient with ourselves at times. You may have been a Christian for many years and occasionally tried to deepen your prayer life and to study the Bible more diligently. However, other things claimed your attention. Your noble aspirations failed and were eventually pushed so far into the background that they were almost forgotten.

If you are determined to refocus on your spiritual goals, don't start by making impressive vows that you know will be difficult to live up to. Learn the secret of living one day at a time and offering your very best to God throughout that day. Even then you will still have a sense of dissatisfaction because your best seems so inferior next to God's holiness and perfection.

The secret of living one day at a time for God is to do so in the strength of the living Christ. Spend time with Christ in the early hours of each day. It will place the entire day in the right perspective.

As you experience every day in His presence, your life will become more meaningful.

Holy God, through Jesus Christ my heavenly Father, I want to live each day in Your holy presence so that I may grow spiritually and become stronger every day.

~ Amen ~

Love ensures a controlled temper

Love ... is not easily angered. (1 Cor. 13:4-5)

People who anger easily, easily explode in fury. That is not the way of true love. Love never despairs about people and does not get impatient with them. When we lose our temper, we lose everything. If all around you people lose their heads and rant and rave with angry outbursts, love will enable you to remain calm, to judge things properly and to make the right decision. This is where Christian love is of immeasurable value in human relations.

The even-tempered person does not harbor hatred and bitterness. Our temper is an innate human characteristic. However, we can channel the nature of our temper. Through the Holy Spirit, it can work to our advantage, depending on how we choose to use it. It is an important sign of spiritual growth to have your temper working for you instead of against you. Love calms your emotions and helps you not to be easily angered.

Lord, my God, I am so quick to anger. I plead for grace to be calm and loving, even under provocation.

~ Amen ~

Are you a Christian?

Follow my example, as I follow the example of Christ.
(1 Cor. 11:1)

How do you recognize a Christian? More to the point: how can others recognize Christ in you? There is much to ponder in these questions, and we should consider them thoughtfully. If we try to answer these questions in all honesty and sincerity, we will need to examine our own lives carefully.

If you profess to being a Christian, it is your responsibility to manifest the characteristics of Christ in your life. No amount of biblical knowledge or church attendance can ever substitute for the image of the Lord in your life. However laudable good works may be, unless they are based on and performed to the honor and glory of Jesus Christ, they lose their impact and meaning.

Your entire life must reflect the love, grace and forgiveness of Jesus so that people will know that you are a true Christian. You should be tolerant and understanding; lead a life of integrity that does not compromise your Christian standards.

When you manifest Christlike qualities in your life, nothing more will be required to confirm that you are a Christian.

O Holy Spirit, I plead that You will grant me the ability to live like Christ more and more each day.

~ Amen ~

APRIL 28

Let wisdom control your life

For the LORD gives wisdom, and from his mouth come knowledge and understanding. (Prov. 2:6)

Your attitude to life reveals whether or not you are in harmony with life. If you are aggressive, you will experience bitterness, frustration and failure. Remember that life is not constantly at war with you.

To experience fulfillment and satisfaction, it is necessary for your life to be controlled by godly wisdom. This wisdom is received from God as you seek for a deeper understanding of Him through prayer and Bible study.

This wisdom affects your whole life. You will begin to see people, circumstances and situations as God sees them. Disciplining yourself to look at life from this godly viewpoint will give you a new sense of values and a purposeful lifestyle.

When you are in harmony with God you will no longer be aggressive because you will not be so easily hurt and you won't pity yourself. You will experience the joy of cooperating with other people through the wisdom God gives you.

Lord Jesus, because, in Your grace, You have given me wisdom, I can discern and know Your will in every situation.

~ Amen ~

The art of Christian conversation

APRIL 29

Let your conversation be always full of grace, seasoned with salt, so that you may know how to answer everyone. (Col. 4:6)

People often underrate the powerful effect of the words they speak. The tone of voice, the timing and the circumstances in which words are spoken are all of cardinal importance. The same words can be interpreted in many different ways.

There are few things worse than seeing someone snubbed by a sharp reprimand or a condescending remark. Experiences like these cause shy or timid people to keep quiet, for fear of being ridiculed or humiliated. Insensitive and intolerant people often speak cruel words that do not take other people's feelings into consideration.

Take a minute to consider how Jesus spoke to the people with whom He interacted. Whether He agreed or disagreed; whether He attacked or defended; whether He addressed friends or enemies; beggars or rulers, there was always a tenderness in His voice. This tenderness is not to be confused with weakness. He spoke with authority, but without being dogmatic. He was always understanding, sympathetic and loving.

Beloved Savior, may what I say always be acceptable to You. Please use my words for Your honor and glory.

~ Amen ~

APRIL 30

The challenge of Christlikeness

Your attitude should be the same as that of Christ Jesus. (Phil. 2:5)

Those who call themselves Christians and walk in fellowship with Christ, must grow in the knowledge and grace of their Lord and Master so that they can become like Him.

To walk in fellowship with the living Christ, and to grow in His grace and knowledge, requires spiritual and mental discipline. You do not need to be a brilliant student, but you must use your mind to the best of your ability and be committed to the service of your Master. Free your thoughts of fear, bitterness, hate, greed, pride and other destructive emotions.

If you feel inadequate to attain these high standards, then in your quiet time, meditate on all the wonderful promises of the Scriptures. The Bible encourages us to develop Jesus' attitude toward life. You must declare yourself willing to follow His guidance unconditionally.

If these challenges sound too theoretical, remember that the Lord has promised His abiding Spirit to all of those who ask for it. Do you accept this challenge?

You are my Comfort, God. Guide me, direct me and teach me.

~ Amen ~

# May

Holy God,
Your unfathomable love knows no bounds!
You love us so much that You sent Your Son
to walk the bitter Way of the Cross, even for me.
Your love knows no bounds! Lord Jesus,
Man of Sorrows, for my transgressions
You were pierced; for my iniquities
You were crushed; the punishment
that brought me peace was upon You;
and by Your wounds I was healed.
How great You are! Your love,
Lord Jesus, knows no bounds.
Lead me to a new level of devotion
and surrender to Your love,
so that You and I may know that
Your suffering was not in vain in my life.
Man of Sorrows, Your love knows no bounds!
We glorify and praise Your holy Name.

~ Amen ~

Surrounded by God's love

"For them I sanctify myself, that they too may be truly sanctified." (Jn. 17:19)

There are probably times when your Christian pilgrimage feels like an uphill slog and a struggle. You may have an deep desire for holiness, to walk daily in the presence of the Lord, to have a meaningful prayer life, to work productively for the Lord. But your enthusiasm fades, your faith grows weak and you begin to wonder if it is worthwhile.

Shift focus and look at your life from Christ's viewpoint. His involvement with your life of faith is more important than your own. He is the one who called you. This divine calling does not depend on your changing emotions. He will bind you to Him with cords of love. When you become despondent, remember that the loving Christ will never change. You still belong to Him, He loves you and He is still your Lord.

Christ's love for you is eternal and unfailing. It doesn't change according to your emotions. When you drift away from Him, He loves you just as much as when you are spiritually dynamic and constantly aware of His divine presence.

I thank You, O Guide, that my changing emotions need not dictate the course of my life. Thank You that Your love for me is constant.

~ Amen ~

MAY 2

You are special to God

For God does not show favoritism. (Rom. 2:11)

God has no "favorites". Whether you are an ordinary person or a celebrity, a leader in the business world or a laborer, whether you are honored by society or considered a non-entity, in God's eyes you are special because you are His child, and He loves you. You are a unique creation of His hand and you have special value in His eyes.

There are so many people who torture themselves with the thought that they are completely unworthy, or that they have disappointed God. They feel unworthy in comparison to others who live a more devoted life. They feel that they have drifted out of the sphere of God's love and trusty care.

Think about when Jesus lived on earth. Christ reached out to both the worthy and the unworthy. He loved His disciples, even though they disappointed Him in His time of despair. He forgave His enemies, even though they nailed Him to a cross.

I know that You live and that You have forgiven my sins. Through Your precious blood I have inherited peace.

~ Amen ~

The extent of Christ's love

MAY 3

Do you show contempt for the riches of his kindness, tolerance and patience, not realizing that God's kindness leads you towards repentance? (Rom. 2:4)

When you consider all the evil in the world and the fickleness of man, you become aware of the full extent of God's love. People ignore Him, they forget His manifestations of grace, they are disobedient to Him, they rebel against Him and they blame Him when things go wrong in their lives. Nevertheless, in His love, God sent Christ to live amongst us and to die for us so that we could be saved and receive eternal life.

No human being would have tolerated the attitude that mankind displays toward God, and still show the infinite love that God does toward His people. Christianity is the only religion based on the great love of God that transcends our understanding.

Acknowledge His merciful acceptance of you as His child. Surrender yourself unconditionally to His Son. Follow Him and live life to the full as He offers it to you (see Jn. 10:10).

Praise the Lord, because He is good. His love is infinite.

God of love, thank You that Your love and grace enabled me to find You. I surrender myself in renewed mutual love to You.

~ Amen ~

MAY 4

In God's loving protection

"Do not be afraid, O man highly esteemed," he said. "Peace! Be strong now; be strong." When he spoke to me, I was strengthened and said, "Speak, my lord, since you have given me strength." (Dan. 10:19)

Worry and fear can so easily become a major part of your life, thus robbing your life of its meaning and beauty. Worry develops into fear, and fear creates more worry and the vicious circle goes on, draining your life of joy and spontaneity.

If your life is being controlled by these negative forces, you need to come to a fresh realization of God's love. Believing that God's love surrounds you and is waiting to be revealed through you is the best antidote for foolish worrying and degenerative fear.

With the help of the Holy Spirit it is possible to be constantly aware of the presence of God. And then you will be able to change your thoughts from negative to positive. Ask God to remove your fear and to replace it with the awareness of His loving presence.

Every time the bullies of fear and worry want to attack you, remember that God loves you and that they have no control over your life.

Holy God, let Your love consume me and ward off fear and worry.

~ Amen ~

The power of God's love

People will oppress each other – man against man, neighbor against neighbor. The young will rise up against the old, the base against the honorable. (Is. 3:5)

Consider everything that happens in the world: it seems as if chaos and anarchy rule in every corner of the world.

This, however, doesn't mean that we need to tolerate the situation. Remember that Isaiah also prophesied the advent of the Savior into this world. He brought light into the darkness of this world. God didn't write off humanity saying, "It serves you right." In Christ Jesus He came to fight against evil. He did this with the only weapon effective enough to overcome the forces of darkness. And it is just as powerful today – godly love.

Even today God continues to shed His love on mankind. It is the Christian's privilege and duty to share this love with others by opening his life to the influence of the Holy Spirit. We must allow Him to work in us so that we can pass God's love on to other people.

There is just no other way of stopping the tide of evil that is threatening society today. Try to become a channel of God's love.

Holy God, make me an ambassador of Your love, sharing it with all those I make contact with in my life.

~ Amen ~

MAY 6

Christ cares for you

Cast all your anxiety on him because he cares for you.
(1 Pet. 5:7)

At times the burdens of life seem overwhelming and all the blessings you've received seem to have vanished. Trials and problems will become a terrible burden if you try to overcome them in your own strength and wisdom. They will drain you of spiritual and mental energy and you will begin to feel that you cannot go on.

It might sound very courageous to state that you can handle everything that life throws at you, but if your spirit is broken and your ability to recover has diminished, you need a real and vital relationship with God.

Consciously sharing the burdens of your life with your Father God, means that you tap into His unfailing power. Then you will be able to stand firm even when the foundations of your life are being shaken.

The glorious truth is that your heavenly Father cares for you. He longs to share your life with you. Every burden and anxiety will be a new opportunity to grow in your knowledge of Him.

Holy Father, I am strengthened and inspired when I consider the great sacrifice of love that You made for me.

~ Amen ~

Christ's way

MAY 7

"Good and upright is the Lord; therefore he instructs sinners in his ways." (Ps. 25:8)

Some people forsake their Christian pilgrimage because they feel unworthy of it. Far too often we meet those who believe that the road is too steep and too difficult and so they deny their faith. Many people get confused or disillusioned in their spiritual life and seem to lose their way.

Never lose sight of the fact that God loves you. Through His unfathomable love, He assures you of forgiveness and redemption. Jesus, who was without sin, took our sins upon Himself to redeem and sanctify us.

He willingly went to the cross and gave His life so that you could be delivered from the yoke of sin. Such is the magnitude of His grace and love!

You are very precious to God and He wants what is best for you. As you follow the guidance of Jesus Christ and walk in His way, you will find peace and consolation. You will grow spiritually and the Holy Spirit will grant you the fulfillment of your deepest desires.

Guide me along Your way so that I can know Your love and find peace and fulfillment in my life.

~ Amen ~

Sincere love

MAY 8

Love must be sincere. (Rom. 12:9)

Most people are disgusted by others whose interest and care prove to be only superficial, and who focus on what is best for themselves. Their friendship is meaningless because their love is insincere.

But you need never doubt the certainty of God's love for you. Love compelled Him to come to this world in the person of Jesus Christ and to suffer and die on our behalf. It was love that gave Him victory over death, and caused Him to ascend to heaven where He intercedes for us.

It was love that urged Him to forgive our sins and to offer us the gift of His Holy Spirit. And so we are able to live a life of hope, faith and assurance, even in the face of disappointment and set-backs.

This world will never know any love greater than that of God in Jesus Christ. He gave us the example of sincere love and He urges us to love as He loved. And He enables us to fulfill His command to love others with sincerity.

God of love, please help me never to lose sight of the greatness of Your love for me, no matter what happens in my life.

~ Amen ~

The gospel in a nutshell

"For God so loved the world that he gave his one and only Son, that whoever believes in him shall not perish but have eternal life." (Jn. 3:16)

Jesus Christ had an exceptional ability to express the gospel in the simplest terms possible so that even the simplest person could understand it, and yet, the profound nature of the message was never lost. The main topic of His message was always the eternal and constant love of God: *"God is love. Whoever lives in love lives in God, and God in him"* (1 Jn. 4:16).

In order to partake of this love, we must first open our hearts to Him, *"If anyone loves me, he will obey my teaching. My Father will love him, and we will come to him and make our home with him"* (Jn. 14:23).

Love for God presupposes obedience to Him, and allowing His Spirit to reign over each aspect of your life.

To declare "God is love!" is much more than a simple and sentimental confession of faith: it requires a particular way of life that confirms your inexpressible faith in the immeasurable love of God.

Holy Father, I rejoice in the knowledge that You are my Savior and Redeemer.

~ Amen ~

MAY 10

Immortal Love

"I have loved you," says the Lord. *"But you ask, 'How have you loved us?'"* (Mal. 1:2)

There are times when hope is destroyed by despair and we feel that all is lost. Then we are inclined to wonder, "How can a God of love allow such things to happen?"

The greatness of God's love for mankind can never be fully grasped by finite human beings. His love is great beyond our understanding.

Who but a loving God and Father would persist in loving people who continually rebel against His goodness? Who but a loving God and Father would have sent His Son Jesus Christ to live among men as a servant and to suffer and die so that we can live?

Who but a God of love would have sacrificed His own life to redeem mankind – those who despised and scorned Him? Who but a loving God would give His Spirit to people enabling them to do even greater deeds than Christ did? This is the loving God who will come again to gather those who belong to Him so that they can live in eternal joy with Him. This is the love of God our Father, our Lord and King!

God of love and mercy, when I consider what You do for me, I can never doubt Your love.

~ Amen ~

The extent of Christ's love

MAY 11

Do you show contempt for the riches of his kindness, tolerance and patience, not realizing that God's kindness leads you towards repentance? (Rom. 2:4)

It is only when you take note of all the evil in the world and take into consideration the fickleness of people that you become aware of the full extent of God's love. People ignore Him, they forget His manifestations of grace, they are disobedient to Him, they rebel against Him and they blame Him when things go wrong in their lives. Nevertheless, in His love, God sent Christ to live among us and to die for us so that we can be assured of salvation and eternal life.

It is highly improbable that any person would have tolerated the attitude that mankind displays towards God, and still persevere in infinite love as God does toward His people. Then we start to appreciate the true meaning of the Christian faith. Christianity is the only religion rooted in the great love of God that transcends our understanding.

Acknowledge His gracious acceptance of you as His child. Surrender yourself unconditionally to His Son. Praise the Lord, because He is good. His love is infinite.

God of love, thank You that Your love and grace enabled me to find You. I surrender myself in love to You.

~ Amen ~

MAY 12

The reassuring love of God

I love the LORD, for he heard my voice; he heard my cry for mercy. (Ps. 116:1)

There comes a time in each of our lives when we urgently need reassurance. A fearful child looks to his parents for comfort and assurance. Even adults need assurance at times. It is important for our peace of mind and the calming of our spirit. Regardless of how self-assured you may be, there will come a time in your life when you will recognize that you have such a need.

But this becomes a problem when you are confronted with hardships and you urgently need advice, yet there is nobody who can assist you in your crucial time. What are you supposed to do then?

The answer to this question is found in the psalm that we read today. God is always there as a refuge and help in time of need. He is always there when you need Him, He always hears when you call to Him from the depths and you can be assured that He answers your prayers.

When you turn to God through Jesus Christ in your time of need, wait upon Him patiently. In His own perfect way and timing, He will lead you along the right path and reassure you of His constant love and care.

O Lord, my God, I love You with all my heart and know that all things happen for my good because You love me.

~ Amen ~

Live in the love of the Father

For you did not receive a spirit that makes you a slave again to fear, but you received the Spirit of sonship. And by him we cry, "Abba, Father." (Rom. 8:15)

A fundamental difference between the Christian faith and other religions is that heathens fear their gods while Christians know that God is love. Heathens try to please their gods because they fear that they will become the object of their terrible wrath. Christians desire to please God because of their love for the One that they call Father.

Nevertheless, the spiritual growth of many Christians is stunted because fear grips their hearts. Even Christians are tempted to yield to feelings of guilt, shame and unworthiness at times. The devil uses all his cunning to discourage them and lure them away from the path upon which Christ wishes to lead them.

While we do not for a moment allege that Christians cannot commit sin or be overwhelmed by feelings of guilt, the important thing is the way in which we handle such situations. Be fully aware of the love that God has for you, confess your shortcomings in prayer to Him, be sincerely repentant and gratefully accept His loving forgiveness. And then continue with your life, victorious and with complete trust in the love of your heavenly Father.

Heavenly Father, I rejoice in the fact that You have called me to be Your child.
~ Amen ~

MAY 14

Our merciful God understands

O LORD, you have searched me and you know me. You know when I sit and when I rise; you perceive my thoughts from afar. (Ps. 139:1-2)

You may want to help someone who has a problem, but you are rebuked for not understanding. This response is often that of people who sincerely want a solution to their problem but would rather suffer then apply the discipline required. It may just be possible that you reveal such an attitude when confronted with problems, and you harbor feelings of depression and self-pity.

Regardless of how you may feel and in spite of the fact that others seem indifferent to your problem, there is One who understands you better than you will ever be able to understand yourself. He knows when you feel, happy or sad, when you succeed and fail. He knows your strengths and your weaknesses.

Never be afraid to pour out your anxieties and fears to Him. When you pray to Him, trust Him completely and share your every worry with Him.

He is always ready to listen and to remove the burden from your shoulders. Remember the words of 2 Corinthians 12:9, *"My grace is sufficient for you, for my strength is made perfect in weakness."*

Holy Lord Jesus, when I share my problems with You, I experience such peace and serenity.

~ Amen ~

God hears your cry for help

MAY 15

In my distress I called to the LORD, *and he answered me. From the depths of the grave I called for help, and you listened to my cry.* (Jon. 2:2)

Many times people complain that they have nowhere to turn in their time of need, or that the person they went to disappointed them. When a problem occurs they feel there is nobody to trust or nowhere to look for help.

The emergency services seem to take a long time to answer your call for help; delays hinder the arrival of help; the right person is unavailable. And so the fear and despair that you face in your time of need are intensified.

The joy of your Christian faith is found in the assurance that Jesus Christ Himself cares for you, and that He will never leave you nor forsake you. Regardless of who and where you are, rest in the knowledge that God loves you and not only hears your cry, but understands your needs better than you do yourself.

Never underestimate the great power of prayer, or God's ability and willingness to answer your prayers. Perhaps you may not always understand His answers right away, but if you trust steadfastly in Him, He will guide you along His path.

Lord my God, in Your protective hands I am always safe from every harm.

~ Amen ~

MAY 16

God's love has no price tag

Peter answered: "May your money perish with you, because you thought you could buy the gift of God with money!" (Acts 8:20)

There are many misled people who think that money can buy them everything. While this may be true of material possessions, it does not apply to things like peace of mind, joy and fullness of life. These are God's gifts of grace that are available to rich and poor.

Everything good and worthwhile that we enjoy is by the grace of God. We don't deserve these things, we cannot earn them and we are not worthy of them. We are who we are and have what we have because of Christ's unfathomable love and grace towards us.

Never take for granted the blessings that you receive from His hand. Even those that seem insignificant are a sign of God's endless goodness and His love for you.

It is impossible to repay the Lord sufficiently for all His goodness and grace, because it cannot be calculated in monetary terms. All you can do is to share His blessings with others. By doing this, you will demonstrate that the love and grace of God are at work in your life.

I want to thank You for the undeserved gifts that You so freely lavish on me.

~ Amen ~

Love without boundaries

MAY 17

And they crucified him. Dividing up his clothes, they cast lots to see what each would get. (Mk. 15:24)

Through the ages people have rejected Jesus. They have turned away from Him, denied and betrayed Him, and have had no time for Him. Nevertheless, in times of need or desperate want, they call upon Him and ask for His help. This is especially true in our era of great haste where people can hardly find time for the Son of God in their busy program – until problems occur!

The marvel of the Christian faith is that regardless of how you treat Christ, He still loves you. You can ignore or oppose Him, you can deny or betray Him, but when you call upon Him in your time of need, He lavishes His boundless love on you and meets your needs.

The crucifixion shows us that the love of Christ knows no boundaries. It is a love so sincere and pure that nothing can withstand it. Whether you are worthy or unworthy, whether you deserve it or not – this is the love that God wants to give to you through Jesus Christ. How, then, can you withhold your love from Him?

Lord, I want to share in the glory of Your love. Fill me with Your love so that I can truly love You as You deserve.

~ Amen ~

MAY 18

When God's love possesses you

He predestined us to be adopted as his sons through Jesus Christ, in accordance with his pleasure and will.
(Eph. 1:5)

If the name and the character of God, as revealed through Jesus Christ, had not been love, it would have been impossible for imperfect and sinful people to enter into a relationship with Him. But, because He is love, He calls you to Him and if you respond to His invitation, your life is miraculously changed.

As the love of God becomes a reality to you, it controls your spirit and you become aware of your unity with the Father. Yet, the love of God that is at work in you is not simply an emotional experience detached from daily life. As you open up your life to His life and influence, the Holy Spirit will enable you to live as He intended: in His strength and in the awareness of His living presence.

When the love of God fills your life and you become thoroughly aware of His divine presence, you experience a feeling of unity with Him. This intimacy isn't something that you can earn through your own efforts. It is a gift from God. It becomes yours when you appropriate it for yourself in faith and with gratitude.

Eternal God, Your unfathomable love is beyond my understanding, yet You have given it to me as a precious gift of Your grace.

~ Amen ~

Love brings life

"We know that we have passed from death to life because we love our brothers." (1 Jn. 3:14)

Everything Jesus was, everything He taught and all He did were manifestations of God's love. People who have not received Him or His teachings cannot understand His emphasis on love. They see love as an emotion that fluctuates according to their every passing mood. They simply do not understand that the power of love overcomes hate and that love can offer itself in years of service without counting the cost. The love of God enriches the lives of everyone who allows Him to pour it into their hearts.

It is possible to experience the love of God firsthand and to allow your life to become a channel of God's love. This is the wisest way we can choose to live. The opposite of loving is hating. This is the path of bitterness, dissension and relationships that are torn apart.

When the love of God is a powerful force in your life and His love reaches out to others through you, your own life is enriched in a way you never dreamed possible.

Lord God, through Your Holy Spirit please do the impossible and enrich my life through the wonders of Your love.

~ Amen ~

MAY 20

All-encompassing love

"The LORD is my shepherd, I shall not be in want."
(Ps. 23:1)

The Palestinians' flocks of sheep and goats were very precious to them. They provided milk, meat and cheese, as well as wool and skins for clothing. Therefore the shepherd took very good care of the sheep. He provided them with pastures and water, protected them against attacks, kept them safely on the right path and searched for the ones that went astray and were in danger of getting lost.

Jesus Christ is your Good Shepherd and you are very precious to Him. He cares for you by providing for your daily needs, by protecting you, by showing you the path of righteousness and by searching for you when you go astray. Then He lovingly brings you back to the safety of the flock.

There is one crucial difference between the Palestinian shepherd and the Good Shepherd. In order to enjoy the care and protection of the shepherd, the flock had to provide for the material needs of the people. Jesus Christ, the Good Shepherd, however, offers you His protection and immeasurable love, and only asks that you love Him in return.

Good Shepherd, thank You for Your loving care and protection.

~ Amen ~

God's unfailing love

MAY 21

"Though the mountains be shaken and the hills be removed, yet my unfailing love for you will not be shaken nor my covenant of peace be removed." (Is. 54:10)

Most of us have first-hand knowledge of the radically changing circumstances of life that often have a dramatic influence on us, and on those whom we love. One moment we experience joy and ecstasy, and then we are suddenly swept into the depths of despair. How often has your world been disrupted by serious illness or death; by failure or financial disaster?

Regardless of unexpected events in your life, you have the assurance of God's love for you. However despondent you may be about the events and circumstances that shake the foundations of your existence, never lose sight of the fact that Jesus loves you with an unfailing, eternal and perfect love. He will deliver you from your burden and your weariness if you go to Him in prayer and faith.

Regardless of the circumstances, or how dark the future may seem, if you take God at His Word and listen to His promises and turn to Him in times of affliction, you will enjoy the blessings of the Lord, as well as His love that drives out all fear (see 1 Jn. 4:18).

Lord, I feel safe in the shadow of Your hand. Thank You for sheltering me when the storms of life are raging about me.

~ Amen ~

MAY 22 — Everlasting arms underneath you

The eternal God is your refuge, and underneath are the everlasting arms. (Deut. 33:27)

Because of the uncertainty of life, you will often experience adversity, and feel as though your world is crumbling around you. This happens when you face major financial setbacks, serious illness, the death of a loved one, or a radical change in lifestyle.

Whatever the negative circumstances may be, no matter how difficult the situation may seem, never lose sight of the fact that God keeps a loving watch over you and that He cares for you. He provides a sanctuary for your battered soul, where you will experience peace of mind amidst the ups and downs of life. He awaits you with outstretched arms, ready to embrace you with His eternal love and endless grace.

In every crisis and every moment of despair, trust in the Lord. Give yourself to Him without reservation and find serenity in His faithful care. Let your prayer of thanksgiving every day be: *"You hem me in – behind and before; you have laid your hand upon me"* (Ps. 139:5). Praise the Lord in the blessed assurance that He will take you in His care – today and forever.

I dwell in You and Your arms keep me safe. I want to live and act through You, because You are my Savior and my King.

~ Amen ~

Take courage

"Have I not commanded you? Be strong and courageous. Do not be terrified; do not be discouraged, for the LORD your God will be with you wherever you go." (Jos. 1:9)

You need to grow beyond that point in your spiritual life where you believe that God desires to penalize you for every mistake you make. To have such a concept of your heavenly Father is to do Him great injustice. It creates a barrier, preventing His loving encouragement from flowing into your life.

God desires for you to live in intimate fellowship with Him; to experience His creative abilities; to express His wisdom in your relationship with others; to draw strength from Him when you are weak, courage when you are discouraged and inspiration when you are despondent. Your heavenly Father does not take pleasure in your failures, but He waits for you to ask Him to meet you at the point of your need and to enable you to become that which He desires you to be.

Then you will not regard Him as one who takes pleasure in condemnation, but as the source of encouragement and inspiration. He becomes your shining light of encouragement when you are downcast. Then He will whisper to you, "Do not be afraid, nor be dismayed."

Father, Your constant encouragement and inspiration keep me strong in You.

~ Amen ~

MAY 24

Precious moments

The LORD is good to those whose hope is in him, to the one who seeks him; it is good to wait quietly for the salvation of the LORD. (Lam. 3:25-26)

When we get unbearably busy, we need to draw aside for a moment of quiet so that we can reevaluate our priorities. It seems so foolish to seek peace and quiet when you are at your busiest. A job needs to be done and it just doesn't feel right to withdraw. Yet the real foolishness is to think that you can succeed without seeking God.

Make time to meet with God. It doesn't have to be for long periods, but learn to treasure those moments and try to extend them. Those are moments in which you can say, "The Lord is with me and He blesses me and I am conscious of His divine presence." Such a time is an oasis where your strength is replenished, and you are spiritually refreshed. It is also the battlefield where the power of Satan is broken.

If you conscientiously set aside time to be alone with God, you will return to your busy life with a sense of balance and peace of mind and the powerful assurance that God is always with you and that He grants you His wisdom, love and grace.

Loving Father, thank You for those precious moments when I am so aware of Your loving presence.

~ Amen ~

Our most glorious life-experience

MAY 25

And to know this love that surpasses knowledge – that you may be filled to the measure of all the fullness of God. (Eph. 3:19)

If you place due importance on your spiritual life, you will remember that wonderful moment when the love of God became a glorious reality to you and you will know that it was the most wonderful experience of your life. It might have been sudden and dramatic, or it could have been a gradual awareness. But the moment when God became a loving reality in your life will always be precious to you.

When the love of God entered your heart and started to find expression through your life, you received a small but important impartation of God's nature. God is love and as you express love, you demonstrate His nature. The realization that God loves you and fills you with His Holy Spirit is an unforgettable experience that increases in richness and depth with time. The influence that God's Spirit has in your spirit is not a once-off experience. It is the sharing of yourself with the God of love, moment by moment through prayer, Bible study, meditation and testifying of His love.

God of love, I praise You for the precious gift of Your Holy Spirit through whom I can experience Your love for me.

~ Amen ~

MAY 26

Love is immortal

Love is as strong as death ... Many waters cannot quench love; rivers cannot wash it away. (Song 8:6-7)

When all the things that people pride themselves in have passed, love will still be constant. Love is powerful. Death seems to reign over all, and yet death can be conquered by love. This love is a deep devotion to the loved one and it frees us from the fear of death. That is why people are even willing to sacrifice their lives for their loved ones.

God's love conquers death. By comparing love to a blazing fire that cannot be quenched by many waters, the writer of Song of Songs compares it to the power of anarchy. Love can conquer chaos. It is priceless, because it cannot be bought. The highest point of our worldly existence is when we discover the love that wards off the fear of death.

Love is the one great thing that helps us believe in immortality. When God's love has entered your life, you begin a relationship against which the onslaughts of time are powerless and that rises above death. God is immortal and God is love; therefore love is immortal.

Thank You Lord God, that love is immortal because You are Love. Help me to share in this love by loving others.

~ Amen ~

We worship a God of love

MAY 27

For he has not despised or disdained the suffering of the afflicted one; he has not hidden his face from him but has listened to his cry for help. (Ps. 22:24)

God is often blamed when families meet with disaster or disappointment, when cruel deeds are committed, when set-backs or failures arise. Then we complain, "How could a God of love allow such a thing?" or "Why has something like this happened to us? After all, we do love God."

One thing we can be very sure of is that our problems have not been planned by God. They may be the result of our willful actions or our own foolishness. God will never do something to harm or injure His children. He loves us so much that He sent His Son to die for our sins.

If it seems as though your whole world is falling apart, you need to consider the part you have played in the situation. Did you go to the Lord with your burdens and problems, asking Him to show you where you went wrong?

If you truly love someone, you do not ignore him when he is in trouble. God feels exactly the same way about you and wants to help you, if you would only turn to Him.

Dear Savior, Your gracious love reached out to save me and relieves me of the burdens of my sin and shame.

~ Amen ~

May 28

God's saving love

To them God has chosen to make known among the Gentiles the glorious riches of this mystery, which is Christ in you, the hope of glory. (Col. 1:27)

There is a generally accepted idea that if we want God to love us, we need to live a good life. We know that God rejoices in the righteous person and that His Spirit enters our lives to change us and conform us to the image of Christ. But the wonder and glory of the Christian gospel is that God loved us while we were yet sinners. Without such a love we would indeed still have been lost.

Faith in the saving love of God is much more than a vague hope. It is something that we respond to instinctively. Even though you are deeply aware of your imperfection and sin, you are also aware that there is a divine power that is beckoning you to a better and nobler life. You also know that you will never be able to reach these virtuous heights in your own strength.

If you are aware of the fact that because of your sins and transgressions, you don't have the ability to live your life as you should, it is important that you accept God's offer to recreate and reform your life. It is important that you allow the Holy Spirit to inspire you with the strength to walk God's way.

Lord, I am sincerely grateful that You loved me while I was still a sinner and that You rescued me from the bondage of sin.

~ Amen ~

God loves you

MAY 29

And we know that in all things God works for the good of those who love him, who have been called according to his purpose. (Rom. 8:28)

People often cannot understand why trials and set-backs happen to them. In many cases God is blamed. Every set-back in life is ascribed to Him.

One of the basic components of Christianity is steadfast faith in the love of God. This love has been proven beyond a doubt in the gift of His Son to a lost world. That is why, in every situation of life, you can put your trust in the wisdom and goodness of a loving Father.

No person can fully comprehend the magnitude of God's love as expressed on the cross on Golgotha. The extent of His love toward sinners is unfathomable and incomprehensible. But without the gruesome events on the cross we would never have shared in God's pure love, and we would never have experienced redemption and deliverance.

When you find yourself facing problems or set-backs, remember that your times are in God's almighty hands. Because of His great love for you, everything that happens to you has a purpose.

Jesus, in the darkest moments of my life I can be assured of the goodness of Your love that lets nothing happen to me by chance.

~ Amen ~

The extent of God's love

"I have loved you," says the LORD. "But you ask, 'How have you loved us?'" "Was not Esau Jacob's brother?" the LORD says. "Yet I have loved Jacob." (Mal. 1:2)

If we should try to count all the ways in which God loves us, we would reach infinity and yet not nearly have managed to name them all. Nevertheless there are many people who still have a problem understanding God's love.

In the midst of personal set-backs and tragedies, in times of national and global disasters, in hardships and disappointments many people hold God accountable for the situation they find themselves in. They question God's wisdom and love for allowing such a thing to happen to them. They repeatedly want to know, "Why?"

They totally miss the fact that all the disasters of this world cannot be ascribed to a lack of love from the Father or the Son, but to the foolishness of man. God gave us freedom of choice and yet we selfishly misuse it.

The love of God is revealed in His abundant blessing, His all-powerful forgiveness, His mercy, His promise of eternal life, His comfort, His gift of the Holy Spirit and above all, the sacrifice of Jesus Christ on Golgotha. Do we need more proof than this?

Lord Jesus, I thank You for the privilege of knowing Your love and forgiveness and mercy.

~ Amen ~

To abide in Christ's love

MAY 31

"As the Father has loved me, so have I loved you. Now remain in my love." (Jn. 15:9)

It is a disturbing thought that we could lose the awareness of the Savior's love. How often do you wake up in the morning and thank the Lord for His love and tell Him of your love for Him? What a blessing it is to wake up in the morning and whisper, "Loving Lord Jesus, I love You with all my heart!"

Jesus Christ has promised that if we acknowledge our dependence on Him, we will be enabled to do things that would normally be well beyond our ability. You cannot reach your full potential until you are united in love with the living Christ. Without Him we can do nothing. By abiding in His love our vision is extended and our strength increased.

Many Christians try to serve the Lord without that all-important love that they need to have for Him. Then it is nothing but slavery. They are active in Christian service, but lack the motivation that comes from love for Christ and their fellowmen.

Diligently develop a greater love for Jesus Christ, so that you can draw closer to Him by the invisible but unbreakable cords of love.

Living and loving Savior, through fellowship by faith I can know Your love and serve You from a heart overflowing with love.

~ Amen ~

June

Holy God, and in Jesus Christ
my heavenly Father: I pray
that You would keep me from
spiritual stagnation; from the danger
of remaining a toddler in the faith.
Thank You that a fountain of
salvation flows from Your throne,
which enables me to grow on a daily basis in all
the spiritual gifts mentioned in Galatians 5:22.
Through the working of the Holy Spirit
keep me from thinking
that I have arrived spiritually
and don't need to grow any more.
Let me keep on growing and bearing fruit
in keeping with repentance,
just like a branch that is grafted into You,
the vine. I pray this in the holy Name
of the source of all things,
Jesus Christ, my Savior and Redeemer.

~ Amen ~

JUNE 1

Your responsibility as a Christian

Instead, speaking the truth in love, we will in all things grow up into him who is the Head, that is, Christ. (Eph. 4:15)

The moment you accept Christ as the Lord of your life, you accept certain responsibilities. Ignoring these cripples your spiritual life and weakens your relationship with the Lord.

When you become a Christian you step into a new life with new values and fresh goals. You no longer live to please yourself, but your goal is Christ. Therefore you deny yourself in your service to others. The good works that you do for others express your faith in the free gift of salvation God has given you through Christ.

If you wish to grow spiritually, there are certain things required of you in your new life in Christ. As a disciple of Christ you have the responsibility of honoring your Lord and pleasing Him. You no longer live only to please yourself. You must be completely obedient to God's will for your life.

In his letter to the Ephesians, Paul urges us to be filled with the fullness of God. Christ should become visible in your life. It is the sacred responsibility of every Christian to constantly grow spiritually, and to reach maturity in faith.

Help me, Lord Jesus, to strengthen my relationship with You so that I can grow more and more into Your likeness.

~ Amen ~

Service yields fulfillment

Today, if you hear his voice, do not harden your hearts.
(Ps. 95:7-8)

There are many people who are dissatisfied with their lives. Some feel that life is merely a monotonous existence; others complain that nothing they do succeeds; others are so busy finding fault with everything that they fail to see the good things in life; and some are interested only in themselves, and so become dissatisfied.

The one sure path to fulfillment is to serve God among His people. There are people who need a helping hand, who seek companionship or a friendly word of advice. There are others who yearn for encouragement or recognition. A few moments of your time can make an immense difference in their lives. Open your heart to God and remain sensitive to the voice of His Holy Spirit. He will touch your heart and guide you toward those in distress.

If you are willing to allow the Lord to use you, you can also know for certain that He will lead you to people He wishes you to serve with His love. The Holy Spirit will give you the right words to say and help you to do all that needs to be done. In this way your life will become dynamic and meaningful.

Fill me with your abundance, O Holy Spirit of God, until my heart overflows and streams towards those who need my ministry.

~ Amen ~

When life disappoints you

JUNE 3

"Why are you downcast, O my soul? Why so disturbed within me?" (Ps. 42:5)

There are people for whom one dreary day follows the next and they wonder whether life is even worth living. They seem to exist without really living. Our heavenly Father does not want us to waste the gift of life on a useless existence. He has given us life to use joyfully and constructively. If you have no plan for your life then your days become aimless and frustrating. That is why it is essential to accept God's plan and will for your life.

Jesus Christ came to give us an abundant life (see Jn. 10:10) and when we accept His will for our lives, He challenges us to enter into a new and satisfying life. This is not a sentimental and vague suggestion but a call to accept the responsibilities of Christian discipleship.

Being a disciple of Christ requires a steadfast conviction of who Jesus Christ is. It means having a firm and unyielding faith in Him. Such faith inspires constructive service to Him. It is through serving your fellowmen that your life gains purpose and meaning.

God, who gives true life, help me to live a life that fulfills Your purpose for me.

~ Amen ~

Reach for spiritual maturity

When I was a child, I talked like a child, I thought like a child, I reasoned like a child. When I became a man, I put childish ways behind me. (1 Cor. 13:11)

Many people's spiritual lives are like riding a rocking-horse: there is a lot of movement, but little progress. There are many people who never achieve mental or spiritual maturity. The grudges of yesterday are carried over to today, poisoning their attitude and embittering every new day given to them by God.

We must forget the insults and grudges that we have nurtured over the years. To say that a grudge cannot be forgotten is to aggravate its poisonous effect. It could cause untold harm to your soul and your spiritual development. Much harm is done to the heart that harbors a grudge.

Your Christlike character should enable you to overcome insults, grudges and vexations that hamper your spiritual growth. Today you have an opportunity to grow by God's grace, to put the negative behind you and to reach for a future of exuberant spiritual growth. If you open your spirit to the influence of the Holy Spirit, a new life will open up to you. He will help you to forgive and forget. Then you can concentrate on those things that lead to spiritual maturity.

Lord, I cannot do anything without You. Fill me with Your Spirit so that I may experience fulfillment in You.

~ Amen ~

Assess yourself

Do not think of yourself more highly than you ought. (Rom. 12:3)

Many people have a poor opinion of themselves and their abilities. When asked to do something, they refuse because they do not think that they will manage it. They turn down invitations because they have no self-confidence. They lead unhappy and frustrated lives because what they believe about themselves is reflected in their way of life.

As a Christian you must assess yourself in the light of God's Holy Spirit. You will then see yourself as you really are, with all your superficial self-pity and self-delusion. This could be uncomfortable and humbling, but if you ask God's forgiveness for the false opinion you have harbored, you will begin to see who you could become through His strength, wisdom and inspiration.

Remember that you were created in the image of God and in His eyes you are invaluable. Then you can assess your life accurately and can, instead of expecting failure, begin to live successfully, especially in your spiritual life. Despair will be replaced by hope. Your goal in life will then correspond with God's assessment of your life.

Jesus Christ, I am eternally grateful to have been redeemed by Your blood. Through You I can inherit eternal life.

~ Amen ~

A balanced inner life

JUNE 6

If any of you lacks wisdom, he should ask God, who gives generously to all without finding fault, and it will be given to him. (Jas. 1:5)

Our lives must be both spiritual and practical. Many people have the misconception that in order to live a truly spiritual life, you need to live in mystical seclusion where the realities of life are ignored.

The things that Jesus taught along the dusty roads of Palestine were deeply spiritual, yet essentially practical. It is extremely difficult to draw a line between that which He regarded as "spiritual" and "non-spiritual". For Him, everything – every thought and deed – was an expression of His relationship with His heavenly Father. Therefore a true Christian does not divide his life into compartments, because everything in life is an expression of his spiritual condition.

A faith that is so "super-spiritual" that it ignores the harsh realities of life, is definitely not inspired by Jesus Christ. His Spirit sharpens the mind and gives it the sensitivity to discern the will of God. Paul Tournier wrote, "I wait upon God to renew my mind, to make me creative, instead of becoming the clanging cymbal that Paul speaks of." The spiritual life touches the realities of every day.

O Spirit, take possession of my life. I pray that You will touch every aspect of my life.

~ Amen ~

June 7

Spiritual maturity

You ... are controlled not by the sinful nature but by the Spirit. (Rom. 8:9)

To appreciate God's greatness and to rejoice in the majesty of His creation elevates the human spirit above the pettiness that results from a limited view of life. When you cannot rise above the pain inflicted upon you by someone's thoughtless words; when your life seems restricted by a lack of opportunities; when you have fallen into a rut from which you just can't escape – then you need to examine the basic reason for your existence.

The direction in which you are traveling clearly indicates what you have emphasized in your life. If you emphasize financial success or social status, you may reach your destination but lose much in the process.

Because you are a spiritual being, your spiritual hunger can never be satisfied with material things. Only a relationship with the Lord can bring true satisfaction. This personal relationship with God is achieved through steadfast faith in Jesus Christ and your willingness to allow His Spirit to live through you. Then you will grow spiritually and your life will have new meaning.

Holy Father, grant me a profound awareness of the importance of spiritual growth, so that I can have a meaningful and sensitive spirit.

~ Amen ~

More Christlike every day

JUNE 8

Instead, speaking the truth in love, we will in all things grow up into him who is the Head, that is, Christ. (Eph. 4:15)

It is a glorious truth that believing in Jesus Christ as your Redeemer and Savior redeems you from your sins. This is the foundation of the Christian gospel. But you should never forget that the process of growth only begins with your decision to follow Him. If you ignore the need to grow, your spiritual life will start to founder in the ocean of disappointment and despair.

In His mercy, God has put many resources for spiritual growth at our disposal, but we should not let these resources become an end in themselves. Fellowship with believers is essential, but if it is not centered on Christ it serves no spiritual purpose. Studying the Scriptures is a source of inestimable inspiration and guidance, but the purpose of such study is to point the disciple to Christ. Good works and helping those less fortunate than yourself are undoubtedly pleasing to God, but they are only the fruits that spring from knowing Christ.

Spiritual growth can occur only when your goal is to be more like Jesus. This should be the desire of every disciple.

Possess me so completely through Your Holy Spirit, O Lord, that my life will reflect Your glory.

~ Amen ~

JUNE 9

Be patient with yourself

But grow in the grace and knowledge of our Lord and Savior Jesus Christ. (2 Pet. 3:18)

When some people commit themselves to Christ the weakness of their character is immediately replaced by strength, and an indescribable confidence fills their life. But after a while the initial wonder and enthusiasm seems to abate, and the heart that was once aflame for Christ starts to cool. This is unfortunately not an uncommon occurrence.

When you surrender yourself to Christ, you become a new creation, but old habits die hard. Therefore it is imperative that young Christians begin to exercise the disciplines that lead to growth immediately after conversion to Christ. The excitement of conversion should be strengthened by the foundation of Bible study, prayer, and fellowship with believers.

Without worship, prayer and Bible study there can be no growth. It is God's desire that you will grow spiritually, but the responsibility for ensuring that it happens belongs to you.

Thank You, Lord Jesus, for starting me on my Christian pilgrimage. With Your help I will work hard at my growth and development.

~ Amen ~

Spiritual or worldly?

JUNE 10

Instead, speaking the truth in love, we will in all things grow up into ... Christ. (Eph. 4:15)

A mistake that people make in their efforts to grow spiritually, is to think that life is divided into two separate parts: the spiritual and the earthly. This also causes a division among people. There are those who focus on spiritual issues, and others who are more involved with what is happening in the world. Unfortunately, there is a tendency amongst the former to regard themselves as superior to the rest.

When a Christian starts to think along these lines, he becomes an ineffective witness. A spiritual person has a lively interest in other people and in what is happening around him. True spirituality is extremely practical. Jesus Himself was a very practical Person. For Him, no division existed between the spiritual and the material worlds. A developing spiritual life should turn the disciple into a balanced and stable person. If you live in the strength of the living Christ, you will be able to understand that all of life should be approached from God's point of view and that everything is subject to His sovereignty.

Thank You that I may know that You are always with me. Through every obstacle You will take my hand. Thank You, Lord.

~ Amen ~

JUNE 11

The danger of complacency

For this reason I remind you to fan into flame the gift of God, which is in you through the laying on of my hands.
(2 Tim. 1:6)

Complacency is a major stumbling block to spiritual growth. When you begin to believe that there is nothing more for you to learn about the Lord and His Word, you have entered a dangerous cul-de-sac that will lead to frustration and spiritual impoverishment.

The Christian life is not a static experience, but is constantly growing in the awareness of God's presence in your life. Sanctification is a process. The seeking disciple finds great satisfaction in making Christ the Lord and Master of his life. He has a yearning to know more about Him every day and to draw closer to Him. This compels him to study the Scriptures and to examine the lives of those who walked the path with Christ before him.

If you have not yet experienced this desire, it could be that you have become complacent and have not responded to the challenge of Jesus. This is the death-knell for spiritual growth. Ask the Holy Spirit to fan the flame in your life again so that you can enter a period of new spiritual growth.

You are my power and my strength. With Your armor I can remain steadfast against Satan's cunning.

~ Amen ~

Be progressive in your spiritual life

JUNE 12

But grow in the grace and knowledge of our Lord and Savior Jesus Christ. (2 Pet. 3:18)

If you have accepted the resurrected Christ as your Savior, it is your responsibility to grow spiritually. To be half-heartedly sentimental in this regard is to court spiritual disaster. In order to have a meaningful spiritual life, you must be disciplined and yield to the will of God.

You should be willing to pray according to the will of God and not according to the demands of your emotions. An active and positive prayer life will transform your thinking patterns, and enable you to think spiritually. You will begin to understand what Paul meant when he said, *"Your attitude should be the same as that of Christ Jesus"* (Phil. 2:5).

To grow in the image of Christ is not a spiritual indulgence that occupies your spare moments, but an absolute necessity if you wish to develop a vital faith. You may be able to maintain the pretense of Christlikeness, but if your spirit is not continually strengthened by the Holy Spirit your faith will not last. Do not stagnate spiritually, but grow steadfastly by the grace of God.

Lord, help me to remain steadfast in faith. Make me brave, strong and courageous, so that my work will carry Your blessing.

~ Amen ~

June 13

A life of fulfillment

For now we really live, since you are standing firm in the Lord. (1 Thes. 3:8)

Knowing that your witness for Jesus Christ is effective is always a source of great joy. It may be something you said; a friendly or kind deed; your support in times of need; a sympathetic ear to someone who was in trouble. The fact that the Lord used you to draw someone closer to Him leaves you with a feeling of humility, awe and fulfillment.

Jesus Christ is still inspiring people through His Holy Spirit to be His witnesses, to proclaim the gospel and win souls for God.

True discipleship is never easy and you will have to overcome many barriers along the way. You will experience setbacks, taste disappointment and have to handle adversity. But you refuse to give up hope. You persevere in your service as Christ did – even when He had to suffer and die.

Seek the Lord in prayer and open your heart to the influence of the Holy Spirit so that Christ can become an essential part of your life. Then you will experience the complete fulfillment that comes only from serving Jesus Christ.

I want to serve You, O Lord, by serving those around me. Help me to be sensitive to their needs.

~ Amen ~

Your responsibility

JUNE 14

"If any of you lacks wisdom, he should ask God, who gives generously to all without finding fault, and it will be given to him." (Jas. 1:5)

Salvation is God's free gift to all who accept it, but if you want fulfillment and joy in your spiritual life, you must work it out diligently in your own life. People who are enthusiastic about their faith derive much greater blessing from it than those who are lukewarm and indifferent about the truths of God.

We need to take the responsibility for becoming spiritually effective. It is useless to plead with God to strengthen your prayer life if you are not willing to give more time to prayer. The desire to become more Christlike is praiseworthy, but unless you are willing to spend time contemplating the life, personality and character of the Lord as revealed in Scripture, your desire will remain unfulfilled.

If you have accepted the Lord's free gift of salvation and have dedicated yourself to Him, you have committed yourself to the responsibility of growing closer to Jesus.

Through prayer and Bible study, spiritual growth is nourished and sustained. These two requirements must be met if you wish to remain true to your Lord and want to develop spiritually.

Lord, my spiritual life is not what it should be. Help me to have the discipline to pray and study Your Word so that I can grow.

~ Amen ~

JUNE 15

Your greatest asset

Timothy, guard what has been entrusted to your care. Turn away from godless chatter and the opposing ideas of what is falsely called knowledge. (1 Tim. 6:20)

As you grow in your spiritual life, you accumulate valuable assets that can only be obtained through experience. Your experience with Christ becomes deeper as you practice a disciplined and meaningful prayer life. You become increasingly aware of the eternal presence of Christ, and the more time you spend with Him, the more real He becomes in your life.

If you find that you are not growing closer to the Lord it is probably because of a lack of prayer and study of God's Word. Spiritual backsliding doesn't usually occur suddenly or dramatically, but laziness and the neglect of spiritual discipline gradually drain your love for the Lord and your loyalty to Him.

As your love for Christ begins to wane, you may find that you begin to defend yourself with explanations and arguments in an attempt to explain the barreness in your life. Christ's love for you and your love for Him is your single greatest spiritual gift. Treasure it in your heart, and your spiritual life will bear much fruit.

Teach me, O Holy Spirit, to focus on the essential matters and not on insignificant things.

~ Amen ~

Live a life of abundance

JUNE 16

Give ear and come to me; hear me, that your soul may live. (Is. 55:3)

Any creature that is deprived of food for long will waste away and die. The body cannot endure the torment of hunger and thirst. It becomes increasingly weaker and then dies. Your spiritual life is also subject to the impact of hunger and thirst and, if not properly nourished, will also wither and die. Just as your physical body depends on good food and water for life and growth, so your spiritual life must be nourished in order to flourish.

Jesus Christ, the Bread of Life, invites us to come to Him and then we will never go hungry or thirsty again. This means surrendering your entire life unconditionally to Him, so that the Holy Spirit can take control and give purpose to your life, thoughts and deeds.

This challenge is as valid today as it was when Jesus said, *"You diligently study the Scriptures because you think that by them you possess eternal life. These are the Scriptures that testify about me, yet you refuse to come to me to have life"* (Jn. 5:39-40). Take up this challenge by turning to Christ and you will experience life in abundance.

Lord Jesus, You are eternal life and I come to You so that I may experience life in all its abundance.

~ Amen ~

JUNE 17

Do you truly wish to change?

Therefore, if anyone is in Christ, he is a new creation; the old has gone, the new has come! (2 Cor. 5:17)

Everyone seems focused on doing something *one day*: the schoolboy dreams of participating in the Olympics, the intern dreams of the day when he will become company manager, the shop assistant lives for the day when he will have his own business.

Christianity is filled with people who will live a more devoted life *one day*, who will practice a more meaningful and more profound prayer life, who will make a thorough study of the Word of God, who will strive to be a better Christian *one day*.

One of the challenges that you will have to face, is whether you truly wish to change or not! There is a world of difference between a desire to change *one day* and to really do so. Before any change can take place, you need to cooperate with Christ. He asks you to submit to His will before He can put new life into your old, rigid life. The moment when you sincerely desire to change, the transformation begins – and that, which you once regarded as impossible, becomes a glorious reality in His strength.

I praise and thank You, Heavenly Father, for the new life that You granted me through Jesus Christ, my Savior.

~ Amen ~

Put Christ foremost in your life

JUNE 18

I want to know Christ and the power of his resurrection and the fellowship of sharing in his sufferings. (Phil. 3:10)

Many of God's servants are so busy working for Him, that they do not have the time for regular quiet times with Him. Few people ever say, "I work for the Lord, therefore I do not have to pray." The truth is rather that they are so active in the kingdom that, gradually and without noticing, their activities become more important than their quiet time with the Father. They are active for God without experiencing the presence and power of the living Christ.

If the vision of what you are trying to fulfill for Him fades, your service will become powerless and ineffective. This is what happens if your spiritual reserves are not regularly replenished through prayer and meditation.

Regardless of the sphere of life in which you are serving the Lord, you must put Him foremost in all your activities. The service that you give to Him must flow from your intimate knowledge of Him. Only when He comes first in all things, can you begin to understand life the way He sees it.

Savior and Lord, help me to put You foremost in my life. You are the inspiration and power of my service to You.

~ Amen ~

JUNE 19

What is a mature Christian?

For if you possess these qualities in increasing measure, they will keep you from being ineffective and unproductive in your knowledge of our Lord Jesus Christ. (2 Pet. 1:5)

Spiritual immaturity is a self-imposed burden that many people carry through life. Many people call themselves Christians because they were born in Christian homes or even because they are part of a Christian society, but they have never fully surrendered their lives to Jesus.

True Christianity starts when you accept Jesus Christ as your Savior and Redeemer. If you want this new life to be meaningful, you need to submit daily to the will of the Lord. He is true to all His promises, but the responsibility to develop a dynamic and vibrant faith rests with you. You may have the desire to pray for a richer prayer life, but unless you are willing to spend more time in prayer it will remain only a desire. You may long to have a stronger faith, but you must make use of the faith you already have.

A committed Christian never stops wanting to become more and more like Jesus. It may sound like an unattainable ideal, but no Christian is fighting alone. Christ strengthens you in your weakness.

Dear Lord, I humbly ask that during my periods of spiritual laziness You will activate me to serve You with diligence and perseverance.

~ Amen ~

Don't get impatient with yourself

Patience is better than pride. (Ecc. 7:8)

Many Christians feel that they should make better progress in their spiritual life. They lament the poverty of their prayer life and their lack of knowledge of the Scriptures. They have a deep desire for a richer experience with the Triune God, but this seems unachievable. And yet they do not realize that their deep yearning to know God better is in itself a prayer that pleases God. He understands your desire for deeper and more intimate fellowship with Him.

As an infant you crawled before you could walk. It takes time to master the playing of a musical instrument. Sanctification also does not happen in a moment. It is the result of a disciplined spiritual life.

Spend time in the presence of God. Examine yourself in His light. Is Jesus Christ more real to you today than a few years ago? Is there greater depth in your prayer life? Does the Word of the Lord play an ever-increasing role in your life? Do not get impatient with yourself because your progress is slow. Walk with Christ day by day, and He will do the rest.

Teach me to walk with You in faith and to please You. I know that those who follow You are one with You.

~ Amen ~

JUNE 21

Love is complete and perfect

When I became a man, I put childish ways behind me.
(1 Cor. 13:11)

Paul says that the spiritual things we see now are like a reflection in a mirror. The modern mirror, with its perfect image, only made its appearance in the 1200s. Earlier mirrors were made of polished steel and only reflected a very vague image.

We see only a vague reflection of the beauty and glory and perfection of God in our lives. Many things seem like mysteries and riddles to us. We see a reflection of God's nature in His creation. We see a clearer reflection in the Word and in Jesus Christ. Even though Christ is the perfect revelation of God, we can only understand it in part because the temporal can never fully understand the eternal. But love will lead us to the place where we will see God face to face and we will know Him as He knows us.

God already knows us in full. He knows how much love there is in our hearts for Him and for our fellowman. One of the highlights of our spiritual growth is discovering that His perfect love is being revealed in and through us.

May the world behold in me the reflection of Your love every day.

~ Amen ~

The blessing of a hungry heart

JUNE 22

"Blessed are those who hunger and thirst for righteousness, for they will be filled." (Mt. 5:6)

God will satisfy those who desire righteousness. Remorse, confession, rebirth, repentance, sanctification and spiritual growth are necessary if we want to be righteous before God (see Jn. 3). To hunger and thirst for righteousness is the sum total of all the Christian virtues.

All people yearn for happiness, but the devoted Christian yearns for righteousness. This begins with confessing and repenting our sinfulness and unworthiness. Then the Holy Spirit leads us to Christ who is the living bread and living water. Those who eat of the spiritual food He provides will never again hunger or thirst.

Christ says, *"Here I am! I stand at the door and knock. If anyone hears my voice and opens the door, I will go in and eat with him, and he with me"* (Rev. 3:20). We will be fully satisfied when we feast at the supper of the Lamb. He paid the price for this feast at Golgotha and all that is required of us is to hunger and thirst for righteousness. Then we will partake of the feast at which Jesus Christ Himself is the host.

Holy Spirit, thank You for leading me to the bread and water of God, so that I need never again experience spiritual hunger or thirst.

~ Amen ~

JUNE 23

Choose your words carefully

There is a time for everything, and a season for every activity under heaven. (Ecc. 3:1)

Truly fortunate are those who can find the right word for the right occasion. There are many people who boast that they are frank, truthful and get to the bottom of things. They say what they think without considering the consequences for themselves and others. They forget that words uttered without love cannot heal a broken spirit, console those who mourn, raise the spirits of someone who is depressed, or give hope to those who are despondent.

Choose your words carefully, and the time and place for speaking them. This is particularly important if the people you talk to cannot reply without fear of reprisal. Sarcasm is an indication of spiritual immaturity and narrow-mindedness.

The words you use reflect your spiritual condition. Petty and bitter words flow from a callous heart. A harsh tone is the fruit of a mind warped by disappointment and frustration. If you want your words to be filled with truth and power, you must live in harmony with the Spirit of truth.

Gracious God, give me the wisdom to choose my words carefully and always to speak with love in my heart.

~ Amen ~

Reflect the presence of Christ

JUNE 24

When Moses came down from Mount Sinai with the two tablets of the Testimony in his hands, he was not aware that his face was radiant because he had spoken with the Lord. *(Ex. 34:29)*

Every picture tells a story, and the same can be said of a person's facial expression. Often it is possible to tell at a glance what kind of person you are dealing with, what emotions he is experiencing and whether you can trust him – simply from looking at his facial expression.

But we often judge people wrongly, and are later disappointed because their perception was based on a misconception. But you never have to doubt a person who has an intimate relationship with the living Christ. It is clear, because the love and compassion of Christ is visible on his face. He looks at you through the eyes of Jesus.

Cultivate an intimate relationship with Jesus and you will become more and more like Him because His Holy Spirit is working in you and reaches out to others through you. Allow Him into your life and allow His love to flow through you to others. Then you will live a life of abundance, which only Jesus can give you (see Jn. 10:10).

Lord Jesus Christ, grant me the privilege of being an instrument of Your peace.

~ Amen ~

JUNE 25

To live an exemplary life

May the favor of the Lord our God rest upon us; establish the work of our hands for us – yes, establish the work of our hands. (Ps. 90:17)

Our daily lives, to a certain extent, influence those we come into contact with, and they tend to judge us. A self-centered, petty and bigoted attitude is usually a reflection of spiritual or emotional immaturity. Such an attitude avoids the challenge Christ presents: to live an exemplary life that reflects His image and love to others.

An exemplary life begins in your heart of hearts for it is there that the divine nature begins its work in you. It is there that you become aware of the presence of the Savior in your life and He helps you to see all that is good and perfect. A truly exemplary life is the result of living in harmony with God through Jesus Christ in the power of the Holy Spirit. Such harmony comes from consistent spiritual growth and a growing understanding of the will of God for your life.

If your character is being developed under the guidance of the Holy Spirit then you will become pure, and your life will be characterized by Christian love.

Dear Lord, may my life be an example of Your goodness.

~ Amen ~

Good intentions

Do not merely listen to the word, and so deceive yourselves. Do what it says. (Jas. 1:22)

If all our good intentions were fulfilled, the world would be a wonderful place. Unfortunately these have no effect if they are not expressed in deeds.

Begin with the simple things. If you planned to write a letter of condolence or apology, do it now. If you are aware of someone who is in need of encouragement and you are in a position to provide it, why not do it immediately? If you don't transform your intentions into actions they will become meaningless.

In the spiritual life, the failure of good intentions is evident in the lives of many people. We will only know in eternity how many people "intended" to follow Jesus at some time or another. They admire, respect and even love Him, but they withhold their full surrender to Him. They keep referring to their good intentions as a way to quiet their conscience.

The Lord expects you, as a Christian, to carry out your good intentions. If you do not, the vision you once had of the good you could do, will die.

Living Lord Jesus, through Your wisdom and power all my good intentions become glorious realities.

~ Amen ~

JUNE 27

He knows and He understands

He did not need man's testimony about man, for he knew what was in a man. (Jn. 2:25)

Just because Christ understands your weaknesses, it doesn't mean that He condones your sins. He, who was tempted like us in all respects, has called you to a life of victory through the strength of His Holy Spirit. Unfortunately, those things which people call "weaknesses", but which are really just sins, rob our spiritual life of its growth and vitality.

As far as Christ is concerned there are no insignificant sins. All sin separates us from the Lord. Christ never glosses over sin. But He does understand human weakness and frailty. He offers forgiveness, and purifies us, saves us, and gives us the spiritual strength to live victoriously.

Christ looks beyond our sin and sees what we can become through the power of the Holy Spirit. He does not see us as struggling, failed and imperfect beings, but as channels of the grace of God who do His will where He has placed us. He knows what people are like, therefore He knows our potential and desires to lead us to the perfection that God has ordained for us.

Holy Jesus, please look beyond what I am and inspire me to be what You know I can be. Let me never hide behind my weaknesses.

~ Amen ~

Make your prayer life effective

JUNE 28

Devote yourselves to prayer, being watchful and thankful. And pray for us, too, that God may open a door for our message, so that we may proclaim the mystery of Christ, for which I am in chains. (Col. 4:2-3)

For many people prayer is something of a drudgery. As a result, their prayer life is powerless and drab – a repetition of hackneyed phrases. They pray to God only in desperation, or out of habit.

True prayer is an exciting adventure that you share with Almighty God, through Jesus Christ. God never gets tired of listening to your prayers. Therefore, your first priority must be to center your life on Him. Develop the habit of tuning your mind and emotions in to Him so that, when you go about your daily tasks, you are conscious of His divine presence at all times.

After you have prayed, it is important to be sensitive to the prompting of the Holy Spirit. In this way you will be guided to discover His answers to your prayers, as He reveals them to you in His own wonderful way.

At all times thank God for the assurance that, in His wisdom and grace, through the living Christ, He will meet all your needs.

I want to bring honor and glory to You for the wonderful privilege of prayer and for all the prayers You have answered.

~ Amen ~

The challenge of Christlikeness

JUNE 29

Your attitude should be the same as that of Christ Jesus. (Phil. 2:5)

Those who call themselves Christians and walk in fellowship with Christ, must grow in the knowledge and grace of their Lord and Master so that they can become like Him.

To walk in fellowship with the living Christ, and to grow in the grace and knowledge of Him, requires spiritual and mental discipline. Serve the Lord with all your heart. Such devotion will free your thoughts from fear, bitterness, hatred, greed, pride and other destructive forces.

If you think you are unable to achieve these high standards in your own life, then consider all the wonderful promises in Scripture. The Bible encourages us to approach life with the same attitude that Jesus had. Look at how He handled human relationship problems and apply His wisdom in your life.

Remember that the Lord has promised His Spirit to all of those who ask for His help to live a godly life. Do you accept this challenge?

You are my Comfort, God. Guide me, direct me and teach me.

~ Amen ~

New life in Christ

Put on the new self, created to be like God in true righteousness and holiness. (Eph. 4:24)

The great foundation of the Christian experience is the fact that the living Christ is in us. It doesn't depend on how you feel and what you do, on your opinions or your emotions. Jesus Christ rules the mind and emotions of those who acknowledge His lordship, who love Him with all their might and serve Him to the best of their ability.

The glorious truth that Christ lives in you should cause a total revolution in your life. Your whole concept of life is enriched and you begin to be aware of the truth of God in its rich fullness. This understanding creates a broader understanding and a spiritual depth and perception that only come from having the Spirit of Christ in you.

The indwelling Christ does not only give you a new approach to life, but also supplies you with the inner power that enables you to live victoriously. Because Christ lives in you, your whole life becomes a new, exciting and satisfying experience. This is God's way leading you to a sanctified life.

I praise and thank You, Lord Jesus for coming to live in my heart and giving me a new outlook on life.

~ Amen ~

July

Gracious heavenly Father,
we worship You as the God of peace.
There are wars, hatred and enmity, violence,
and confusion all over this world.
We plead: Lord, grant us peace in our time.
There are misunderstandings, suspicion,
and antagonism, and hatred fills the air.
Make me an open, receptive channel,
always ready to be a bearer of Your peace.
Let my eyes see what You see: the beautiful,
the good, and the pure around me.
Let the words of my mouth testify
of Your love in my heart, Your light in my mind,
Your peace in my soul. O Prince of Peace,
on behalf of a strife-torn world,
I lift my hands to You in prayer:
Give us peace, O Lord!

~ Amen ~

JULY 1

I am with you!

"When you pass through the waters, I will be with you; and when you pass through the rivers, they will not sweep over you. When you walk through the fire, you will not be burned; the flames will not set you ablaze."
(Is. 43:2)

It requires great faith and a strong character to be able to work through adversity and disappointment. Many seemingly strong people eventually double up under their burdens and break down.

The Lord never promised that our lives would be free from problems just because we choose to serve Him. But He did promise to be there for you at all times and to help you over life's hurdles. Knowing that you don't have to tackle the afflictions of life on your own is a comforting and reassuring thought.

To ensure your peace of mind, it is important to hold on to the truth that Jesus is the living Christ. He comes to live in you through His Holy Spirit, and is closer to you than any one else. Because He was able to rise above the worst that people could do to Him, He is now at your side every step of the way.

When problems mar your view and put you under pressure, turn to Christ. He is your heavenly companion. Overcome your problems in the peace of His presence.

Thank You, omnipotent Father, that I can say with confidence that You are with me day by day.

~ Amen ~

Peace in the storm

JULY 2

You will keep in perfect peace him whose mind is steadfast, because he trusts in you. (Is. 26:3)

If you allow your thoughts to dwell on the things that happen in the world today you run the risk of being caught up in a maelstrom of hatred, bitterness, and fear.

God has given you a wonderful gift to help you to remain steadfast and to overcome personal fear. He grants you His eternal life. Because He is love, He plants His love in your heart and gives you the peaceful assurance that this love can never be destroyed – not even if all the forces of hatred come against you.

When your faith threatens to fail, He gives you the power to believe that all things are working for the good of those who love Him. If you surrender your life to Him, His peace will be your glorious possession at all times and under all circumstances (see Jn. 14:27). This peace is the direct result of trust. When your faith in God is sure, you possess an inner calm that brings balance to your life. Put God first in all things and you will know His peace and joy even in the most trying circumstances.

Almighty God, with You at the center of my life I fear no storms, not even those that become hurricanes.

~ Amen ~

JULY 3

"I know for certain!"

"Peace I leave with you; my peace I give you." (Jn. 14:27)

The peace that Jeus offers His followers differs in nature and content from human peace: His is peace with the King of the universe. With this, Jesus gives us another perspective on life: He wants us to look at life through God's eyes. Then worldly things suddenly do not seem to be that important. What God thinks of you and how you relate to God form the foundation for your peace.

We need His peace in our daily life, in our homes, and our world, but most of all, in our innermost being. There is often discord in the world around us. There are times when the peace in our homes is disturbed.

The Lord does not want us to stress about what is happening around us. He promised, *"The Lord blesses his people with peace"* (see Ps. 29:11).

If only, in all the confusion, we would look away from the world and look up to God who is waiting to grant us His peace and love, it would make a radical difference to our lives.

Prince of Peace, Jesus my Savior, thank You that I know for certain that You have not only redeemed me, but that You also grant me Your heavenly peace.
~ Amen ~

God's peace is unfailing

For who is God besides the LORD? And who is the Rock except our God? (2 Sam. 22:32)

Often when people experience a need or a problem, they look for help or advice. They may look for tangible help from a friend, they may look for relief in the form of some medicine or drug. Yet others will seek the assistance of professional counselors.

If you find yourself in a difficult situation, don't underestimate the power and love of God. In your efforts to solve your problems and relieve your difficulties, don't forget that the only true and effective remedy is to be found in the encompassing love and tender care that Jesus Christ gives to all who turn to Him.

Human effort always falls short. Complete healing flows from an absolute and unconditional trust in, and surrender to, the living Christ. It doesn't matter what your problem is, the only lasting solution is to be found in the unfathomable love which God, through Jesus Christ, bestowed upon mankind.

Never be too proud or too afraid to turn to Jesus. Lay all your problems at His feet. He gave His life to you and will grant you the healing balm of His peace.

I want to hold on to You, Lord, when the storm winds blow and I feel so insecure. Grant me Your peace.

~ Amen ~

JULY 5

Peace in prayer

Devote yourselves to prayer, being watchful and thankful. (Col. 4:2)

There are many people whose lives are ruled by anxiety, worry and fear. They worry about their future, their family, country and the world. Violence, crime, civil unrest, terrorism or political and economic instability are often the cause of their fears and anxieties.

Paul provides the answer to such fears when he says, *"Do not be anxious about anything, but in everything, by prayer and petition, with thanksgiving, present your requests to God. And the peace of God, which transcends all understanding, will guard your hearts and your minds in Christ Jesus"* (Phil. 4:6-7).

There is nothing that you can do in your own strength to solve your problems. Jesus said that without Him we can do nothing, but He also said that in God, all things are possible. Regardless of how difficult, or how bleak the future may seem, your peace of mind is assured if you seek Jesus in prayer. Prayer and meditation, accompanied by praise and thanksgiving, is the only infallible method to ensure that you will be able to confront and handle life.

How wonderful, Lord, that I can come to You when I am filled with sorrow and when I repent of my sins; that I can come to You through songs of praise. Thank You for hearing my prayers with love.

~ Amen ~

Peace be with you!

JULY 6

For the sake of my brothers and friends, I will say, "Peace be within you." (Ps. 122:8)

Discord and dissension are always unpleasant. They cause bitterness, hurt feelings and resentment that can cause immeasurable damage to human relations.

It is foolish to add to the flood of problems in our world today by getting involved in bitter quarrels or by harboring grievances. To enjoy the good that life has to offer, it is essential that you live in peace with your fellowman, and you can only do that if you are living in peace with yourself. Broken relationships will leave you confused and insecure and could cause you to act contrary to your true nature – to your own detriment as well as that of others.

During His earthly ministry, Jesus had to handle a tremendous amount of adversity and enmity. He endured mockery, hatred, humiliation, unfair criticism and rejection. Nevertheless, He never allowed circumstances to get the better of Him. And this was only possible because He was at peace with God, with Himself and with all people. Christ offers you His peace. Accept it and express it through your life and you will experience a life of harmony and peace.

Savior, because I found You, my life is filled with an indescribable peace.

~ Amen ~

JULY 7

Grace and peace to be found only with God

I lie down and sleep; I wake again, because the LORD sustains me. (Ps. 3:5)

Insecurity leads to uneasiness and confusion. If you are insecure about your future, if you are not sure about the next move of your competitor, if you are all alone in the dark of night imagining that you heard footsteps you could develop an uneasy combination of anxiety, concern and confusion. How do you prepare yourself to handle any situation that could arise, so that you can ensure a peaceful and safe life?

History reveals that people who walked intimately with God, found hidden resources of strength to overcome adversity. Those who have an unflinching faith in the living Christ will not waver or break under attacks. Those who put their trust in the all-surrounding love of Christ will not give in to the icy touch of fear.

The same Christ who hushed the wind and stilled the storm at sea, is calling out to you today, "Be strong and courageous; do not be afraid!" Put your trust in Him and see for yourself how His love and grace cause the storms in your life to subside.

O Lord, I'm so insecure about the things that are happening around me. Help me to trust You in the midst of the storms of life.

~ Amen ~

Jesus' steps of peace

JULY 8

As they talked and discussed these things with each other, Jesus himself came up and walked along with them. (Lk. 24:15)

Regular quiet times are precious times in which you become aware of God's presence. Put away preconceived ideas of how He will make Himself known to you, and simply wait on Him in silence, knowing that He is nourishing your soul.

Even though your quiet time with God brings peace to your heart, the demands of everyday life could make you lose sight of what you gained in your time with Him. Maintain contact with Jesus in the course of a busy day by noticing Him in unexpected places. Let Him speak to you through the voice of your fellowman or strengthen you as someone serves you. He might look to you through the eyes of a lonely stranger, seeking companionship. See His beauty in the smile of a child. A brief prayer for passers-by in a busy street can bring His presence very close to you.

As you obey Him in seemingly trivial matters, He will become increasingly real to you and you will hear His soft footsteps at unexpected times and places.

Help me to see You today in all kinds of unexpected places. And as I do, help me to grow in awareness of Your presence.

~ Amen ~

JULY 9

The road to peace

Jesus said to the woman: "Your faith has saved you. Go in peace." (Lk. 7:50)

Worry, doubt and fear are notorious for the destructive influence they can have on a person's emotional and spiritual well-being. People who were once stable and confident collapse into confused wrecks through constant worry.

How often have you been in a situation that you could not handle because you could not see any solution to your problem? You feel incompetent and totally hopeless.

In order to remain standing strong in such circumstances and to avoid the potholes of foolish actions, it is important that you strengthen your faith in God. It is essential that you trust Him unconditionally and commit yourself and your situations to Him. Allow Christ to show you His path for your life.

Perhaps you think that this is beyond your ability – and you would be right. But all things are possible with God. The closer you stay to the living Christ in every difficult situation, the more you will find that He lovingly guides you through every circumstance, along the path of His peace.

I believe in You and therefore I experience peace that passes all understanding. Thank You that nothing is impossible with You.

~ Amen ~

God speaks out of the storm

Then the LORD spoke to Job out of the storm. (Job 40:6)

It is by God's grace that we can spend time with Him and experience His peace and find the pressures of life ebb away. He helps us put our priorities in proper perspective again. In the silence we experience God's guidance and an increasing awareness of His love.

If life is filled with pressure and tension, you will find comfort in knowing that God spoke to Job out of a storm. It is futile to suppose that God can reveal His will to you in the hurly-burly of modern life.

God is willing to guide you in the midst of the storms of life if you live in obedience and submission to His divine will. You can be conscious of His living presence at all times. He is with you in all circumstances to listen and to help. Feverish activity is no barrier to Him. Turn to Him and you will find that He is waiting. Then the bustle of your life will become focused and by His grace you can do all things to His honor and glory.

Help me, loving Master, not to let the business of every day overwhelm me. Help me to see You in the storm.
~ Amen ~

JULY 11

Inner strength

I pray that out of his glorious riches he may strengthen you with power through his Spirit in your inner being.
(Eph. 3:16)

It is amazing how many people go to great lengths to develop their body and increase their knowledge, yet totally neglect their spirit. A mean-spirited person has not yet really experienced the beauty and mercy of God's love. Not only does he miss one of the greatest experiences of life, but also ignores a source of strength and inspiration that cannot be found on earth.

When you become conscious of God's indwelling presence, you not only experience His strength, but also become aware of the beauty and richness of life itself. If Christ lives in you, His strength and beauty will permeate your life. Opening your life to the gracious influence of the Holy Spirit fills your life with blessings, the greatest of which is the awareness that Christ dwells in your spirit.

Christ, who lives in you, wants to reveal Himself through you to the world around you. If He is in control of your life, you develop a new sense of meaning and your whole life will be filled with His glory.

Almighty God, through Your power my life gains new perspective and meaning. Thank You.

~ Amen ~

The center of Christ's peace

JULY 12

"Peace I leave with you; my peace I give you. I do not give to you as the world gives. Do not let your hearts be troubled and do not be afraid." (Jn. 14:27)

Few people can honestly say that they do not long for peace of mind and inner tranquility. The general insecurities of life today create a deep-seated sense of insecurity.

Many of those who suffer seek professional help. The psychiatrist's couch and tranquilizers have become a common way of living. Others turn to drugs and alcohol to try to ease the pressure. Yet others give in to despair and simply go through the motions of living from day to day.

The only proven way to handle the pressures and tensions of life is through faith that is steadfastly grounded in the living Christ. Your relationship with Him cannot only be a fleeting acquaintance. You need to live in constant unity with Him. Hold on to Him in all circumstances, talk to Him, regardless of how desperate your situation might be, trust that He is always with you. Even though you may find it difficult to understand His peace, you will recognize it when it fills your heart, and helps you overcome all your fears.

Prince of Peace, please help me to first turn to You in everything that happens to me today.

~ Amen ~

JULY 13

Your search for peace

To whom he said, "This is the resting place, let the weary rest"; and, "This is the place of repose" – but they would not listen. (Is. 28:12)

In stressful times people tend to become weary. This is especially true in our society where so much is made of achievement and results. People of all ages struggle with tremendous pressure.

Yet, in the midst of our rushed lives, Christ invites us to, *"Come to Me, all you who labor and are heavy laden, and I will give you rest"* (Mt. 11:28). Yet so few people respond to this invitation. We much rather look for man-made solutions to help us cope with the pressures of life. It is incomprehensible that people hesitate to turn to Jesus Christ and to accept the only true peace, which He so freely offers.

Regardless of how busy you are, you must make time to withdraw from the demands of each day and spend time quietly at the feet of the Master. Focus on Him and His love. In the quietness, be strengthened by His peace. Regardless of how demanding your life might be, you will experience strength, peace and tranquility as the Holy Spirit ministers His healing work in your life.

I have such a need of Your rest, Lord. Help me to be strengthened in the peace of Your presence.

~ Amen ~

When fear overwhelms you

JULY 14

But Jesus immediately said to them: "Take courage! It is I. Don't be afraid." (Mt. 14:27)

Fear destroys the peace and harmony of innumerable lives. Thousands of people live in the shadow of fear from morning to night, and even when they are asleep, fear still remains active in their subconscious.

The fruits of fear emerge in all spheres of life. Irritation leads to strained and broken human relationships. When you are afraid, you are not open to reason and can become antagonistic. Fear also manifests in illness and in avoidance of responsibilities.

Fear has a thousand faces. Jesus, however, knows them all, and He tells you not to be afraid. Remember that He commands His disciples to banish all fear, regardless of external circumstances and pressures.

You and the world you live in still belong to God, even though it might not always seem so. Your heavenly Father has not abandoned or forsaken you or His world. He promised the Holy Spirit to those who love Him. If this Spirit takes possession of your life, destructive fears will no longer have any hold on you. And then you will begin to know the joy of a fearless life.

When Your Holy Spirit fills my life, Lord my God, there is no space for destructive fear.

~ Amen ~

JULY 15

Quiet time is essential

"Come with me by yourselves to a quiet place and get some rest." (Mk. 6:31)

Many people fail in their Christian walk because they try to find substitutes for the time that they should spend alone with God. They might work very hard for God, and become involved with many good causes, rather than spending time alone at the feet of God.

Many people find it uncomfortable to be alone with God because there they become aware of their weaknesses and imperfections. While it is true that God is a just Judge, He is also your loving Father. In your quiet time alone with Him, you not only discover who you are, but also who you could become through yielding to His abiding Presence. When you meet with God in quietness you begin to triumph over self-centeredness and weakness.

If you want to live a life of triumph through Jesus Christ, you will have to learn to become quiet in the presence of God and allow His Holy Spirit to bring peace to your heart and soul. Then you will learn to fulfill His will for your life.

It is wonderful to seclude myself and to be quiet with You in these busy times, my Lord and my God.

~ Amen ~

Peace with an instruction

JULY 16

Again Jesus said, "Peace be with you! As the Father has sent me, I am sending you." (Jn. 20:21)

As the pressures and fears of life increase, people become more and more tense and more pressured by the demands on their time. The more technology develops to meet the demands, the more the tempo of life increases.

This pressure cause people to snap, and the results are seen in irritation, angry outbursts, pettiness and eventually the breakdown of the foundation of our Christian faith – love! In order to meet the tremendous demands of modern life, you need to meet quietly with God on a regular basis. There you find His peace and also His command to become a peacemaker for God.

In His strength you will find that you are able to handle the pressure without snapping under the tension because the Holy Spirit fills you with the peace of Jesus Christ. You can then pass this peace on to others and they will also begin to live under the influence of the peace of Jesus Christ.

Lord, the pressure has become so severe that I don't know what to do. Reveal Your will for me in these hard times.

~ Amen ~

July 17

The power of silence

This is what the Sovereign L<small>ORD</small>, the Holy One of Israel, says: "In repentance and rest is your salvation, in quietness and trust is your strength, but you would have none of it." (Is. 30:15)

Many people talk a lot or are always busy with all kinds of activities. They seem incapable of calming down or keeping quiet. When they cannot find something to do they feel guilty and begin some insignificant or unnecessary task.

Constructive activity is, of course, necessary, but it is equally important to withdraw from the mad rush of life and focus on what is really important. Most of us find it easier to tackle the problems of everyday life than to meditate on the goodness and greatness of God. Yet even a short time spent in God's presence will bring a new sense of balance and strength to your life.

When we draw aside with God we tend to carry the frustrations of our day with us. And because we spend our quiet time thinking about them, we leave just as frustrated as when we began.

When you enter the presence of God, spend time reading your Bible and perhaps some kind of devotional book that will help you focus on the Lord. Then you will be filled with His harmony and peace.

I thank You, my Lord and Master, that I can meet You when I come to You in quietness.

~ Amen ~

Be silent before Him

JULY 18

Be still before the LORD, all mankind, because he has roused himself from his holy dwelling. (Zech. 2:13)

Although our souls long to be silent in the presence of God, as the parched earth longs for rain, we often find it hard to be quiet before Him.

Life is full of challenges. There is so much to be done and the clamor around us often drowns the still small voice in our hearts – the voice of wisdom and conscience. We tend to rush around and surround ourselves with noise because we fear what we might hear in the silence. Yet entering into the silence of God's presence brings many rewards.

Your mind might try to convince you that there are more urgent things that need to be seen to and that sitting quietly is a waste of time. With the help of the Holy Spirit, persevere even though it feels strange at first. Don't feel guilty about the things that are being left undone.

As a result of time spent alone with God, you receive strength and guidance to reach your full potential and His presence will become a creative force in your life.

I become silent in Your presence, O most Holy God, so that I can clearly establish your will for my life, and receive the strength to obey.

~ Amen ~

JULY 19

Quietness with God

"Be still and know that I am God; I will be exalted among the nations, I will be exalted in the earth." (Ps. 46:10)

We live in a fast-paced world. We become so tired and storm-tossed with all our efforts that we become frustrated and find it difficult to handle the pressure. We lose perspective and our world seems to unravel at the seams.

One tried and tested method of controlling a life that threatens to spin out of control, is to set aside some quiet time with God. When Christ was at His busiest He often withdrew from the multitudes to the quietness of the hills of Galilee to become still with His Father.

We struggle to enter this quietness with God because we lack focused concentration. It requires time and commitment to practice being quiet with God. You need to be patient with yourself, persevere and concentrate. Get to know God from His Word. Don't be in a hurry or lose patience. God is waiting to meet with you in the quietness and to impart His peace to you. Your responsibility is to calm down and to focus on Him with your heart and your mind. It does require discipline, but you will receive the great reward.

Holy God, I come to You in quietness, to be filled with the beauty of Your peace.

~ Amen ~

Peacemakers for God

"Blessed are the peacemakers, for they shall be called sons of God." (Mt. 5:9)

We are shocked when we see the violence, unrest, bloodshed and lack of peace in the world. But slowly we become conditioned to accept it as part of life. What can we do to contribute positively to peace? We can bless everyone we meet with a quiet prayer for peace.

But first you need to find peace for yourself. Come to God with your storm-tossed life and become quiet before Him in prayer. Listen to what He wants to say to you through His Holy Spirit. In the time that you spend with Him, rid yourself of all fear, prejudice, anger and grievances against your fellowmen. Walk the road of forgiveness and reconciliation and allow His love to fill your heart. It is love that brings understanding, harmony and peace.

Become a peacemaker for Christ through praying sincere prayers for peace. And His peace will begin to flow from your life in ever-widening circles. This will merge with the peace flowing from all of God's children praying for peace, and will rise up to His throne of grace. He hears and He will answer.

Prince of Peace, I pray that You would help me to bring Your peace into the lives of others.

~ Amen ~

JULY 21

The safe haven of Jesus' love

The LORD is my rock, my fortress and my deliverer; my God is my rock, in whom I take refuge. He is my shield and the horn of my salvation, my stronghold.
(Ps. 18:2)

We all seek shelter at one time or another. It may be the security of your home, or a shelter against the wind and rain. In times of war, shelter is sought against falling bombs. Our spiritual and intellectual faculties are also often ravaged by the storms of life. We all need a safe and secure haven where we can find shelter from these storms and be protected from devastating emotional consequences.

Regardless of what happens to you, and the seriousness of the situation in which you find yourself, place your trust and faith in God at all times. Even when it seems as though everything is lost, entrust yourself to the love of Jesus Christ. God has promised never to fail you nor forsake you. With this assurance in your heart, you can face the future with confidence. With the confidence that the Holy Spirit grants you, you will know that, regardless of how dark the road ahead may seem, Christ, with His love, is your shelter and safe haven.

Thank You, my Lord and my God, that I find shelter in You and that I will be safe now and for all eternity.
~ Amen ~

God is a refuge

Is any one of you in trouble? He should pray. Is anyone happy? Let him sing songs of praise. (Jas. 5:13)

When we face a crisis, prayer is sadly often a last desperate act when all other efforts have failed. But right through Scripture we are encouraged to turn to God and call on Him in prayer in every circumstance in life. Paul said, in everything by prayer and supplication, that we must let our requests be made known to God (see Phil. 4:6). Yet, the average person looks for human solutions first, rather than considering God's loving invitation. Over and over He promises His assistance and grace to those who call on Him in their times of need.

Not only does Scripture mention the Lord's many invitations, but it also records numerous examples of the wonderful ways in which He answered the prayers of believers.

Regardless of what the crisis or need in your life may be, lay your problem confidently before Him. Trust Him unconditionally and place yourself in His care. Believe in His ability to guide you along the road that He planned for you. Obey Him and He will transform your crisis into an opportunity.

Father, I am experiencing a crisis. Give me Your peace so that I can see things from Your perspective and make the right decisions.

~ Amen ~

JULY 23

Slow down

But I trust in you, O LORD; I say, "You are my God." My times are in your hands. (Ps. 31:14-15)

Some people are so busy that they have no time to really live. Every minute of every day is jam-packed and the mere thought of slowing down fills them with horror. But people who have learned to slow down often achieve more with their lives.

It is really a matter of establishing your values. There are people who say that they have no time to develop a meaningful prayer life. They are so busy working – even working for God – that they regard it as a waste of time to spend time quietly in His holy presence.

Spiritually mature people know the importance of time spent in prayer, Bible study, contemplation of God, and other spiritual disciplines. If you determine the course of our life in partnership with God, you will achieve more of lasting value than those who anxiously drive themselves on from minute to minute. To be still in the presence of God can be the most constructive and productive part of your day.

Holy Spirit of God, make me aware that the most precious moments of my life are those that I spend in Your presence.

~ Amen ~

The power of Christ's peace

JULY 24

Let the peace of Christ rule in your hearts, since as members of one body you were called to peace. And be thankful. (Col. 3:15)

Many people are fearful and insecure because of the constant changes in the world. They long for peace and stability. In spite of all our achievements and technological developments there is still so much famine, poverty, violence and dissatisfaction in the world. And so sober, right-minded people become more and more anxious.

But before peace and stability can be established in this world, people need to open up their hearts to Christ so that He can change their lives. If Christ is to gain control over the affairs of humanity, people first need to commit their lives to Him. By asking Him to take control of your life and acknowledging Him as your Lord and Master, submitting your mind, words and actions to His control, you contribute to peace on earth.

When we surrender ourselves to Christ, we see life, people and situations through His eyes, and we can handle life in His strength. This creates peace that passes understanding and this is where the solution to the world's problems is to be found.

Your peace gives me stability in this uncertain world. Your peace gives me strength to seek solutions to problems. Fill me anew with Your peace.

~ Amen ~

JULY 25

Peace in the midst of chaos

But in keeping with his promise we are looking forward to a new heaven and a new earth, the home of righteousness. (2 Pet. 3:13)

In times of crisis some people lose all courage and hope, and threaten to collapse in what they perceive to be a lost battle against insurmountable problems. To everyone who believes in Him Jesus offers a life of abundance. This promise encompasses your life here and now and through all eternity. Because Christ conquered sin and death, He has prepared a place for all the faithful in eternal glory in the kingdom of God.

If you surrender yourself to Him, the Lord will give you His Holy Spirit. His Spirit gives you the ability to handle life's problems successfully in the certain knowledge that He will not forsake or abandon you. As Paul says, *"If God is for us, who can be against us?"* (Rom. 8:31).

Whatever your circumstances may be, remember that Jesus is constantly at your side to guide and help you. Place your trust in Him as He leads you, and remember that He is continually guiding you toward God's eternal kingdom where there is only harmony and peace.

Beloved Lord, I know that this life's struggles and problems will soon pass, and then I will enter into the eternal peace of Your kingdom.

~ Amen ~

Freedom and peace through Christ

Jesus replied, "I tell you the truth, everyone who sins is a slave to sin." (Jn. 8:34)

Many people are slaves to destructive habits; they have no control of their tongue and they lead lives that pander to the baser human instincts. And to add to the burden, many people are driven by bitterness and animosity. Sin is a harsh taskmaster and it robs life of all beauty and liberty.

Unfortunately many people have accepted this type of bondage as a way of life. Because they've always lived an inferior spiritual life, they are oblivious to the freedom and peace that Christ offers.

The Word promises, *"Therefore if the Son makes you free, you shall be free indeed"* (Jn. 8:36). The liberty that Christ offers is a unique experience through which we are set free from the destructive influence of sin. When you accept Christ as your Lord and Master, you enjoy a new freedom, and a new pattern of life begins. All bitterness dissipates in His glorious love. The Holy Spirit sanctifies your thoughts, words and actions. The freedom that Christ gives spans your whole life and is the only way to find freedom and joy.

By doing Your will my life will be filled with peace that lasts forever.

~ Amen ~

JULY 27 — God's perfect timing

I am the Lord; in its time I will do this swiftly. (Is. 60:22)

Never get impatient when God does not react to your despair on your timetable. It is only when you live in perfect harmony with Him that His perfect timing becomes clear to you. You look at the problems from the perspective of time, while God sees them from the perspective of eternity. Remember that God's timing is always perfect even though it may not always seem that way to you.

Very often we find it difficult to accept God's timing. Sometimes we rush into His presence with an urgent request, commanding Him to act before disaster strikes! Then we tend to act in our own strength – and the consequences are usually disastrous.

If you want to keep in step with God's timing, the first and most important requirement is to develop a meaningful relationship with Him. When His will becomes of primary importance to you, then you become aware of His perfect timing. You will no longer be ruled by panic-stricken thoughts or actions. Then you will know the quiet contentment and peace of mind that are the portion of those who have implicit faith in God.

Lord, You are omnipresent. When I lose all hope, You are there. You will even deliver me from death. Thank You that I know that my life is safe in Your hands.

~ Amen ~

Christ's peace – my inheritance

Peace I leave with you; my peace I give you. I do not give to you as the world gives. Do not let your hearts be troubled and do not be afraid. (Jn. 14:27)

This world's peace is but a poor reflection of that which God gives to His children. To claim this inheritance, we first need to be in the right relationship with the testator. We must become His children by accepting Him as our Father in faith (see Jn. 1:12). Then we need to seek His perfect will for our lives, accept it, and obey Him (see Lk. 22:42).

The peace of God is the most wonderful peace imaginable: it enables us to live in peace with God, ourselves and our fellowmen. The peace of Christ is unique and totally different from what the world calls peace. It affects every area of our lives. The peace of God is constant and does not change according to our moods.

Such peace banishes worry, because that is the weapon the devil uses to undermine our peace. It prohibits fear, because fear is the enemy of all peace. But above all it requires a steadfast faith in Jesus Christ, the source of this peace.

I praise and thank You for the peace that overcomes the fear and anxiety in my life.

~ Amen ~

Piety and peace

JULY 29

On that day HOLY TO THE LORD *will be inscribed on the bells of the horses, and the cooking pots in the* LORD'S *house will be like the sacred bowls in front of the altar.* (Zech. 14:20)

Piety is a word that often has a negative connotation. A person described as pious is considered to be hypocritically virtuous. Nevertheless, piety is a virtue that is very close to the heart of God. True piety is not an act to impress people. It is conduct that flows from a life anchored in God, a longing to give expression to His will and allowing His Spirit to take the initiative in every situation.

This means that your life will become holy. Zechariah had a vision of piety when he prophesied that the ordinary, everyday things will be engraved with the words, "Holy to the Lord."

There is a rich reward for those who desire to live for God. To consciously live in God's presence sanctifies one's whole life. The power that He imparts to your spirit enables you to obey Him. The more intimately you love Him, the more you understand Him and the life He has called you to.

If you include God in every moment of your life, He will give you His peace. Then you will find a precious treasure that comes only from God.

Grant me, O Lord my God, to live in holiness before You, in a way pleasing to You.

~ Amen ~

Jesus can help you

JULY 30

"The LORD your God goes with you; he will never leave you nor forsake you." (Deut. 31:6)

Many people find their lives being shaken to the foundations when set-backs come their way. A serious illness; the death of a loved-one; old age; financial needs; confusion and worries about an unsure future: all these things can create a feeling of despair, despondency, hopelessness and futility.

In such times you must turn to Christ and put all your trust in Him. The Lord who lived, died and rose for you, sees you as very precious and He cares for you. Christ has assured you that He will not leave you nor forsake you and you can put all your trust in Him (see Heb. 13:5).

In moments of weakness and despondency, when it seems as though ominous thunder clouds overshadow your life, remember that Jesus Christ is with you. Talk to Him; put your trust in Him completely; tell Him about your fears and anxieties. Ask Him to give you strength to carry your burden.

Trust Him unconditionally and you will find that you can handle your problems. The Lord Jesus becomes involved in your life and He fills your life with His peace!

With You by my side, Lord, I will never give in to despair. Thank You for filling my life with hope.

~ Amen ~

JULY 31

With Christ into the future

Do not be a terror to me; you are my refuge in the day of disaster. (Jer. 17:17)

There are many people who worry about the future of the world. Startling changes occur all over the world. We are living in a world that is changing at a very fast pace and only God knows what the future holds for us.

All through the ages the world has gone through great upheavals. And people who derive their strength from their faith in God have always managed to handle it and survive. The same God is still with us today: *"Jesus Christ is the same yesterday, today and forever"* (Heb. 13:8). He promised, *"I will never leave you nor forsake you"* (Heb. 13:5).

If you want to experience peace of mind when looking at the future, it is important to put your faith in Jesus Christ. Surrender yourself unconditionally to His love and care. Allow Him to prescribe the pattern of your future.

You will experience problems and obstacles, but you will be assured of safety on the journey ahead. Your companion in these ever-changing times will be the living Christ who is faithful till eternity.

O God, abide with me as I face the future with You by my side. Help me to accept every change with fortitude.
~ Amen ~

August

Holy Jesus, full of love and grace,
there are many people who urgently need
Christian love: The aged, the sick,
the poor, the mournful, the lost,
children, and young people.
We so easily profess our love for You,
but when it comes
to our neighbor, we fail dismally.
Give us eyes to see the distress around us;
Give us ears to hear their plea for help;
Give us a mouth to preach
Your message of love;
Give us hands that will do
something to alleviate sorrow;
Give us a heart that will have
compassion for the pain
and suffering around us.
You are indeed our Perfect Example
in everything; be so in this as well, Lord Jesus.

~ Amen ~

Friendship under pressure

Demas, because he loved this world, has deserted me and has gone to Thessalonica. Crescens has gone to Galatia, and Titus to Dalmatia. (2 Tim. 4:10)

Nobody knows why Demas, Crescens and Titus parted company with Paul, and whether the parting was temporary or permanent. Even among Christians relationships are sometimes tense. To ignore such difficulties increases the tension, and to allow them to continue can destroy the spirit of unity.

Even in the most intimate relationships it is necessary to respect personal privacy. Times when a person wants to be alone with God must never be invaded by another, regardless of the intimacy of the relationship. It is only by respecting each other's individual needs that friendship can grow in strength and beauty.

Prayer, love and honesty can relieve tension within relationships. Pray for God's blessing upon the person who has become estranged from you. You might discover something in your own life that has contributed to the tension. Through the wisdom of the Holy Spirit, you will be able to handle the situation correctly.

Through prayer, love flourishes, and if dialog is necessary, let it be tempered by love. Speak only the truth in love.

Wondrous Lord, teach me to appreciate friendship and to cherish it.

~ Amen ~

AUGUST 2

Do you have a human relations program?

How good and pleasant it is when brothers live together in unity! (Ps. 133:1)

It is rewarding to understand people and maintain healthy relationships. In some cases this is relatively easy. So much depends on the disposition of other people: with some it is easy to start a conversation and their pleasant personalities make interaction easy. But not all people are like that.

Some people are abrupt and difficult and they seem to derive pleasure from making things unpleasant for others. Ignoring such people does not solve the problem. And you might miss the opportunity to know a unique, although difficult, person. Handling the issue constructively requires patience and sympathetic understanding. You need to give others the opportunity to talk, and even if what they say hurts. You will discover that behind the rough exterior and apparent rudeness there is a heart that yearns for love and friendship.

Once you have discovered this, you can help meet their need. Then you have discovered the special art of making friends out of potential enemies.

God of grace and love, in Your strength I strive to understand all people so that I can live in peace with them.

~ Amen ~

Discover the good in other people

AUGUST 3

Finally, brothers, whatever is true, whatever is noble, whatever is right, whatever is pure, whatever is lovely, whatever is admirable ... think about such things. (Phil. 4:8)

Some Christians inadvertently attempt to do the work of the Holy Spirit. They continually try to convince people of their sins and constantly point out their mistakes. When a Christian spends all his time condemning others, he misses the crux of the Christian gospel: that all people can become new creatures in Jesus Christ.

A sincere Christian will see the "new person" in a completely different light. He no longer sees the fallible side of the human personality; the side with all its weakness, unpleasantness and sin; but he starts to understand the good that there is in people he meets. He accepts the good points, even in those who do not yet follow Christ, and develops an appreciation for everything that is "right" and "noble".

When a Christian is looking for the good in his fellowmen, he will discover that people gradually respond to that which is being expected of them. When you expect the best in a person, you will often find that that person accepts the challenges of Jesus, the living Christ.

Lord and Savior, through Your Holy Spirit, I increasingly see the good in my fellowmen.

~ Amen ~

Let your love be practical

AUGUST 4

Let us not love with words or tongue but with actions and in truth. (1 Jn. 3:18)

True love is not easily fathomed. Yet, of all the human emotions, it is the most profound and dynamic. It is difficult to put the unique qualities of love into words. Unsuccessfully we try to express it in intelligible language. Compassion, friendliness, tenderness, and many other beautiful words do not succeed in describing the power and strength of love. We tend to reduce love to mushy sentimentality, thus diminishing this dynamic force, making it powerless and ineffective.

The basis for true love is identification with the loved one. It is to experience his or her joy, sorrow, temptations and disappointments. True love involves sacrifice, and often sorrow. The true quality of love surpasses sympathy and sentimentality, and manifests itself in loyalty and faithfulness.

Love in action is more than doing good deeds, although these are an expression of love. Pure love is profound and unselfish and embraces the faithfulness and noble principles that enrich the mind and heart of a person. It cannot be bought, borrowed, begged or stolen. It is precious above all things.

O Holy Father, enable me to love without counting the cost.

~ Amen ~

Love is practical and sincere

This is how God showed his love among us: He sent his one and only Son into the world that we might live through him. (1 Jn. 4:9)

Jesus Christ was deeply practical. Study the miracles and healings that He performed and the love that He showed and you will note that together with the profound spirituality of His ministry, He had a truly practical nature. When He raised Jairus's daughter from the dead, He told her parents to give her something to eat.

True love and caring requires more than mere words: it calls for action. It requires of you to support someone in prayer, but also to do something practical to show how much you love the person, even if it causes you inconvenience. Visiting a patient in hospital or an elderly person in a home for the aged, sending a card or a letter to someone who is going through difficult times, phoning someone who is lonely; all these things are practical expressions of love and they will bring joy and happiness to the lives of others – as well as to your own.

By demonstrating your love for others in a practical way, you follow the example that Jesus set for us. In this He is our example, because His love exceeds all other love.

Holy Jesus, help me to love others with a love that is sincere and practical.

~ Amen ~

To love one another

AUGUST 6

Make room for us in your hearts. We have wronged no one, we have corrupted no one, we have exploited no one. (2 Cor. 7:2)

The core of the Christian faith is the love of God. It was His love for the world that compelled Him to send His Son, Jesus Christ, to the world to die for our sins. Christ's whole life was the epitome of love in visible form. He fulfilled the words that no man has greater love than that He lay down His life for His friends. The Son of God died for us because of love. Jesus said that the greatest of all commands is to love God and our fellowmen with all our heart.

If you are obedient to the commands of the Lord, He will reveal His love through you. His Holy Spirit will urge you to seek out those who are alone in this world and to bring them comfort in the Name of the great merciful God. Allow Christ into your life and let His love compel you to serve those who are lonely, and people will be able to see the Lord in you.

Love is the cornerstone of your faith. Build upon it diligently and bring comfort and encouragement to others. By doing that you will honor and glorify God.

Lord, may Your Holy Spirit move me to love others the way You love them.

~ Amen ~

Toward a better understanding of people

AUGUST 7

In all your ways acknowledge him, and he will make your paths straight. (Prov. 3:6)

There are many people whose cheerfulness may impress you, but you don't see the deep sorrow or frustrated heart concealed behind their smiles. People who are lonely often feel dejected. To feel that nobody loves you or needs you, can fill your heart with pessimism. To have fought but known only defeat, could make a person dejected. These and similar factors all contribute to depression that can overwhelm your heart.

While some people do not hesitate to tell the world of their depression, others hide their feelings behind a smile. It calls for a sensitive and perceptive person to grasp the true situation. How different it would be if we took the time to understand people before we comment on their conduct. There would be less criticism and condemnation and much more love.

One of the Christian disciple's characteristics is an understanding heart. To be able to penetrate the mask of pretense and offer people understanding and comradeship, is one of the glorious results of the Holy Spirit in your life.

Grant me an understanding heart, O Father, so that I may love people more sincerely.

~ Amen ~

Tomorrow may be too late

AUGUST 8

Do not withhold good from those who deserve it, when it is in your power to act. (Prov. 3:27)

Christian kindness must be a sincere and true reflection of the love of Jesus Christ. He acted wherever He saw people in distress. He did not turn people away or tell them to come back later. His life demonstrated His own words, *"Just as the Son of Man did not come to be served, but to serve, and to give his life as a ransom for many"* (Mt. 20:28). And when He had to lay down His life, He performed His greatest deed of love without a moment's hesitation.

That is the example we must follow if we want to live a life that conforms to Christ's. Too often we hesitate when there is a need. We are embarrassed or we fear becoming too involved in other people's affairs. We may be willing to offer temporary assistance, but the prospect of permanent involvement deters us from making ourselves available.

A person with a problem needs help now; tomorrow other issues may arise that will make it too late. Jesus never hesitated to help others. Should we do otherwise?

Holy Spirit, lead me onto paths of service in the name of Jesus and equip me to help others in their distress.

~ Amen ~

What does your "caring" mean?

"'Look after him,' he said, 'and when I return, I will reimburse you for any extra expense you may have.'" (Lk. 10:35)

When true sympathy is offered to others, it consoles a sorrowful heart and comforts those who are discouraged. To be deeply touched by the misfortunes of others enriches your spirit, because true sympathy stirs profound emotions and helps you to understand the sadness and pain of others.

The Good Samaritan experienced such emotions when he "took pity on" the victim of the robbers at the roadside. However, he did not merely sympathize, but did something practical to ease the suffering of the unfortunate man.

How sympathy can be practical is not always immediately clear. Sometimes it seems that all you can do is to say, "I feel with you." Even that is better than saying nothing. A short visit with the person in trouble will help tremendously. Merely showing that you care is already a consolation.

Praying for the person can bring healing to his heart. To know that they are receiving support in prayer can be of great consolation to people. And the one who prays is enriched because he is a channel of God's healing grace and comfort.

Make me an instrument of Your healing grace, O Lord, so that I will be a blessing to all who are in distress.

~ Amen ~

AUGUST 10

Spare a moment for others

"Don't be afraid." And he reassured them and spoke kindly to them. (Gen. 50:21)

Friendliness is a priceless quality. In the merciless world in which we live people are often too busy with their own interests to even think about someone in distress. The pressures and demands of the business world cause people to become hot-tempered and impatient tyrants. They constantly pursue greater success but drive their colleagues to the edge of despair. They might become very wealthy, but at the expense of their peace of mind. They may have great authority, but they lose the respect of the people with whom they work.

If you want to live a fulfilled life, start by caring about the feelings of others. Show an interest in the welfare of your colleagues. Be sympathetic when they make mistakes, because no one is perfect.

Follow the example of the Christ who was sympathetic and understanding to all people. It will give you great satisfaction and peace of mind to know that you are supporting someone on the difficult path through life. There can be no greater reward than to know that you are carrying out the work of the Lord.

Holy and merciful Lord, in Your strength I will strive to assist my fellowman in need.

~ Amen ~

Washers of feet

After that, he poured water into a basin and began to wash his disciples' feet, drying them with the towel that was wrapped around him. (Jn. 13:5)

Much has been said about love and humility. Many have tried to explain how they should best be applied in life. Despite all the philosophizing, the fact remains that the world still desperately needs true love and humility to be demonstrated on a daily basis so that the ills of this world may be healed.

Jesus, in His ordinary and down-to-earth way, provided us with a practical demonstration of what is required by God. On the eve of His crucifixion He washed His disciples' feet, demonstrating love through servanthood. He proved that the humble will be exalted and that love can conquer all things.

In these days there is a great need throughout the world to allow the humility and love of Jesus to conquer pride and hatred. Instead of washing each other's feet, we tend to berate each other. The path to lasting relationships is paved with humility and love. For this Christ died on the cross. Let us therefore become washers of feet for Christ.

Holy Master, we want to take You at Your word and follow Your example. Grant that there will be more sunshine in this world because of my humility and love.

~ Amen ~

Do not judge

AUGUST 12

Do not take revenge, my friends, but leave room for God's wrath. (Rom. 12:19)

Many people pass judgment because of their preconceived ideas. When dealing with complex situations, it is important not to be influenced by hearsay or wild speculations.

Avoid judging others, as you cannot really understand their circumstances because you have not lived through their exact situation. To walk in the shoes of the one who is being judged gives you wise insight. Judgment belongs to God. If you attempt to judge, you will create conflict in your innermost being, because you burden your mind with condemnatory thoughts. If you do judge, is it because of love and concern for the person or from a desire to see him humiliated? If you form your opinion with the attitude of Jesus Christ, your love will have constructive and edifying healing qualities.

Before passing judgment, consider your own shortcomings and weaknesses. Think of the love and wisdom of your Savior when He said that the one without blame should cast the first stone. Judgment, if truly required, must be tempered with love and compassion.

Help us to glorify Your name in everything we do. Please soften our hearts and help us to show compassion toward others.

~ Amen ~

The dynamics of the spoken word

A word aptly spoken is like apples of gold in settings of silver. (Prov. 25:11)

A single word can have a major impact on a person's life. How we speak is therefore of utmost importance. Some people have a special flair for words and, by choosing the right word at the right time, can make a big difference to another person. But a wrong word and bad timing can have a devastating effect on someone's life.

At times people yearn for a word of encouragement or compassion, and an expression of love can brighten their day. A word of praise or good advice is never wasted; even constructive criticism or a concerned reprimand can be beneficial.

The most important thing is that, through the power of the Holy Spirit, you should choose your words wisely and determine their timing with care. Be sensitive to the person you talk to. Avoid needless flattery and, equally important, heartlessness. Always be sincere in what you say and speak with the love of Jesus Christ in your heart. In this way you will enrich not only the life of the person you are talking to, but your own life too.

Your name is so holy and great. Help me, Lord, to never say or do anything that will disgrace You.

~ Amen ~

AUGUST 14

Love that is kind

And the Lord's servant must not quarrel; instead, he must be kind to everyone. (2 Tim. 2:24)

Kindness is the good nature of love. There are many Christians who are good people, but who are somewhat unkind. They believe passionately in God, but would like for people who differ from them to burn at the stake. Many good people have a critical spirit. Many good Christians would have sided with the Pharisees against Jesus, regarding the woman who was caught in adultery.

The kindness of love strives for justice to prevail – toward God and your fellowmen. In essence, faith means loyalty and reliability, which arise from the love of God. This kindness seeks the best for your fellowmen, regardless of what they may do to you. All bitterness and vengeful thoughts are put behind you, and you live in peace with everyone. After all, this is what God expects of us.

Those who follow Christ wear the badge of kindness. We will only succeed as witnesses for Him in this world, if we do so with kindness and Christian love. Our kindness must be evident to all people; they will then seek the source of our kindness and they will find Jesus.

Lord Jesus, let my love always be accompanied by kindheartedness, so that I can spread Your image in this world.

~ Amen ~

Love is the key

Bless those who persecute you; bless and do not curse. (Rom. 12:14)

When you or someone you love suffers as a result of someone else's actions, it is easy to harbor hatred in your heart instead of completely forgiving the person responsible. You cannot pretend to forgive someone while still holding a grudge against him. Forgiveness demands that the slate be wiped clean so that you can start anew without any anger in your heart.

This is, of course, humanly impossible, but with God the impossible becomes possible. The first step on the road to forgiveness is prayer. If someone has wronged you or a loved one, pray for the wrongdoer. Ask God to bless that person and to give you the grace to do so. Pray that His love will take away all bitterness so that the healing balm of His peace can flow through your heart. Then you will find that the obstacle of bitterness has been removed, and the love of God will enable you to grant unconditional forgiveness.

The love of Jesus Christ has achieved victory over evil in its most barbaric forms. Let this same love cure you from your bitterness.

Jesus, my Redeemer, help me to forgive in love as You forgave me in love. You redeem me also from the bitterness of an unforgiving spirit.

~ Amen ~

AUGUST 16

What do we owe one another?

Let no debt remain outstanding, except the continuing debt to love one another. (Rom. 13:8)

If we consider the matter carefully, we will realize that we all have so much to be grateful for to the Lord. God's mercy and love for us are infinite. He granted you life and the freedom of choice to do with it what you wish. Even the most dejected person will, if he ponders the matter seriously and honestly, inevitably find something for which he can thank and praise God.

How do you prove your gratitude to God for His bountiful grace in your life? No money, no material possessions, no hours of service sufficiently recompense Him for His love – a love so great that not only does He shower you with blessings, but He also sacrificed His life for you.

Love can never be repaid sufficiently, because it is precious and priceless. You cannot measure the magnitude of it; it cannot be weighed to determine its value. Love can only be passed on and shared.

Here you have the only way in which you can acknowledge the great love that God has for you: by sharing it with each person whose path crosses yours.

O Holy Spirit, help me to understand the lesson of true love as God has taught it to us through Jesus Christ. Grant that my every thought, word and deed will be an act of love for You.

~ Amen ~

Be careful in your judgement

"Do not judge, or you too will be judged." (Mt. 7:1)

Have you ever noticed a criticizing person's attitude towards life? His disdain of his fellowman is reflected in his refusal to see any good in his neighbor. It does not matter what noble deed is performed, he will always come up with some disparaging remark. The critic finds it extremely difficult to give sincere praise and encouragement and is therefore usually an embittered person.

Destructive criticism from a non-Christian is bad enough. But when a person calls himself a Christian, and yet instead of encouraging, motivating or building up others, discourages others at every possible opportunity, you will see the tragedy of failure in the Christian faith.

As a disciple of Christ you are called upon to live positively and constructively. If you are in company where disparaging remarks are being made about someone who is not present, it is your Christian duty to defend the absent person.

Loving Lord Jesus, if I have to criticize, make me a constructive and loving critic at all times.

~ Amen ~

Keep your communication channels open

AUGUST 18

And do not forget to do good and to share with others, for with such sacrifices God is pleased. (Heb. 13:16)

So many relationships lapse into a monotonous rut because communication dies. The disintegration of communication with the Lord is a sure way of pulling away from Him.

When prayer becomes the repetition of meaningless phrases piously spoken, true communication dies. Then prayer becomes words without meaning, and fellowship with Christ is no longer enriching.

Meaningful communication does not happen easily or as a matter of course. It has to be cherished and developed. Husbands should share their experiences with their wives, because by talking to each other love and understanding are strengthened.

In prayer and communication with the Lord, in the good deeds we do in His name, we are making sacrifices that please God. Talk to your Redeemer as you would to a friend; tell Him of your hopes and fears; tell Him that you love Him. This will keep your communication with others alive and strong.

O Holy Spirit, prevent my communication with God and with others from becoming meaningless. Make the communication of my prayers meaningful, so that my human relationships can also be healthy.

~ Amen ~

Live to bless your fellowman

AUGUST 19

"Love your neighbor as yourself." (Mt. 22:39)

It is so easy to become self-centered. You talk about what you want and what you own, until you feel that this world was created especially for you. If this happens, something of inestimable value dies within you and people will no longer seek your company. Self-centeredness can destroy the beauty of your character.

If you want to live a full and satisfying life, you need to love and serve other people. Jesus emphasized this when He said, *"For whoever wants to save his life will lose it, but whoever loses his life for me will find it"* (Mt. 16:25). Bless others, and you will be amazed at how the quality of your own life improves.

If you want your life to have meaning and purpose, you need to lose yourself in someone or a cause that is greater than yourself. It is at this level that Jesus Christ reveals Himself as the Great Inspirer of people like you and me, and who said, *"Love your enemies and pray for those who persecute you"* (Mt. 5:44). To bless in this way in the power of Christ, is to discover a full and satisfying life.

In Your power and through Your grace, Powerful Savior, I bless my fellowman and, in doing so, experience a full and rich life of service.

~ Amen ~

August 20

Love can rule the world

All of you, live in harmony with one another; be sympathetic, love as brothers, be compassionate and humble.
(1 Pet. 3:8)

The world is filled with the noise of accusations and counter-accusations. Nation against nation; organization against organization; person against person. The turbulent noise of the sounds of war resound over virtually every country. Aggression becomes the rule rather than the exception.

There is not much that ordinary people can do to bring peace to the world. But every Christian can start somewhere. Start in the neighborhood where you live and work. It costs nothing to be courteous and friendly, obliging and kind. It is not difficult to offer sympathy to someone who is deeply troubled. That is what Christian love is all about: caring for others.

If you are willing to allow Jesus to use you in the service of your fellowmen, you can make an enormous impact on your community. If every Christian did this, love would rule the world. Open your heart to the Holy Spirit and start serving others with love. You could start a flood of love that will inundate the world.

Lord God, let Your love cover the world and rule it by conquering the hearts of people.

~ Amen ~

Establishing healthy relationships

AUGUST 21

Be kind and compassionate to one another, forgiving each other, just as in Christ God forgave you. (Eph. 4:32)

There are certain things in life that you should guard against: complacency, selfishness, foolish pride, unhealthy thoughts, ridicule and a disparaging attitude that inflicts pain on other people.

By hardening your heart against appeals for help and forgiveness, you could harden your spirit and distort your character. Some people harden their hearts toward people less fortunate than they are because of meanness or pettiness; or they think that by offering understanding, love and possible financial aid, they would be exploited.

The way to overcome an indifferent attitude is to approach life with the attitude of Jesus Christ. Then you will have sympathy for, and understanding of, the frustrations of those less fortunate. You will begin to think and act constructively.

A compassionate attitude will help you develop meaningful and lasting relationships; it allows the Spirit of God to work through you and, once again, bring you to the realization that only through being a blessing to your fellowman can you receive the love and blessing of God.

Sometimes we are so uninvolved. Help us, Lord, to comfort those who are filled with sorrow. Help us to support them in neighborly love.

~ Amen ~

Be loving!

August 22

He did not need man's testimony about man, for he knew what was in a man. (Jn. 2:25)

People are very interesting. Each person is so unique that life will never be monotonous as you get to know different people. In your relationships, your attitude will determine their attitude toward you. Accepting the truth of this will make life much easier and more interesting for you.

If you are constantly criticizing others, you erect barriers that friendship finds hard to overcome. If you regard others with contempt, you will taste the bitter fruit of loneliness. Your attitude toward others need not be expressed verbally, because people can feel intuitively what you think of them.

For the sake of your own peace of mind and happiness, it is important that your attitude should be inspired by the Holy Spirit. The most constructive way to live, is to love people. Bitterness vanishes, shyness is overcome and inferiority is replaced by self-confidence. Loving others will not only enrich your own life, but will draw people to you who will enrich your quality of life.

Through the love of God you will understand the people around you better and serve them better too.

Jesus of Nazareth, please teach me to speak words of love in truth.

~ Amen ~

Speaking the truth in love

The lips of the righteous know what is fitting, but the mouth of the wicked only what is perverse. (Prov. 10:32)

Some people are very careless with regard to what they say. They couldn't care if what they say is appropriate or whether it deeply hurts the person they talk to. They take pride in the fact that they honestly say what they think. They tread on the feelings of others mercilessly and thoughtlessly. These people normally live a very lonely life because others steer clear of them as much as they possibly can.

People who are aware of the powerful impact words have, use them to help, encourage and heal. When unpleasant truths have to be expressed, do so with gentleness and tenderness so that it will alleviate the pain of what is said. When, as a Christian, you are required to speak frankly, it will be wise to spend time in quiet prayer first. Pray for the guidance of the Holy Spirit so that you can receive the grace to handle an unpleasant task with sympathy, dignity and love. As a "righteous" person, willing to say the "right thing" in a difficult situation you can trust the Holy Spirit to assist you in your task of love.

Lord, guide me to tactfully encourage and help people to grow into Your image and likeness.

~ Amen ~

Unconditional love?

It always protects, always trusts, always hopes, always perseveres. (1 Cor. 13:7)

Life is largely a matter of give and take. Unfortunately some people demand things that cannot be given. Love cannot be demanded – it must be earned. Parents cannot demand love from their children simply because they gave birth to them. Love creates love, and as a child is nurtured in love, he learns to respond in love.

Elderly people tend to fall prey to self-pity; instead of giving love, they demand the impossible. If they would only develop an attitude of love, and pray for those who help them, others will provide for their needs with great joy.

Many of the beautiful things that enrich our lives come from the ordinary people who learned to love their neighbors. Even though their love is often accompanied by sacrifice, the joy they experience far exceeds the sacrifices. Those who are motivated by the love of Christ, serve the world around them with the love that fills their hearts, asking no reward in return.

Those who make demands and insist on rewards may enjoy temporary benefits, but those who give in the spirit of God's love, discover the rich and permanent blessing that God bestows on them.

God of grace, thank You that I can unconditionally love and serve others, because I follow Your example.
~ Amen ~

The challenge of love

AUGUST 25

(May you) know this love that surpasses knowledge – that you may be filled to the measure of all the fullness of God. (Eph. 3:19)

One of the most difficult commands Jesus gave us is to love one another as He loves us. The question that immediately arises is: How can I love a cold-blooded murderer? How can I show love to someone who has harmed me? How can I love a child-molester?

In our own strength this is impossible, because human nature clings to the principle of an eye for an eye and a tooth for a tooth. However, history has proven that these are not the solutions. The only way to restore reason and stability to our world, is through the all-embracing, all-powerful love of God that can soften the hearts of the most hardened of men.

Jesus needs people who will demonstrate His love by praying for all people, regardless of how appalling their deeds may be. The Evil One has never had the power to conquer the power of prayer and love that comes in the Name of Christ. It is your privilege to be part of this miracle.

Loving and merciful God, help me set aside all personal feelings and to offer myself to be an instrument of Your love in this afflicted world.

~ Amen ~

Reach out to others

AUGUST 26

"Whatever you did for one of the least of these brothers of mine, you did for me." (Mt. 25:40)

Let us thank God for people who take pleasure in helping others. No task is too insignificant for them, and they delight in doing good unobtrusively. They do not seek any reward, except for making life richer and easier for others. Such people are usually happy. To forget about yourself in the service of others is the path to a full and satisfying life.

Now is the best time to start. Find somebody who is in need. You will not have to look far, because the world is full of people who are destitute. A lonely person might welcome friendship; someone who is confused will appreciate a good and understanding listener; a lonely person will welcome visitors with all his heart; a single parent will be grateful for a responsible child-minder so that she can go out for an evening. There are so many different ways in which to help. While you are helping others, you will receive a rich blessing as your reward. Every good deed that is done in the Name of Christ bestows a blessing on both the donor and the receiver. Most of all, it brings glory to His Name.

Lord and Master, make me sensitive to the needs of others.

~ Amen ~

Caring for others could cure the world

AUGUST 27

Each of you should look not only to your own interests, but also to the interests of others. (Phil. 2:4)

Selfishness and self-centeredness stand out as a major cause of poor human relationships. Regardless of where it manifests itself – whether in the national or international arena, or in our relationship with one another – a lack of caring and consideration for each other places a blot on society.

Jesus' whole life was devoted to caring for others. His love for people was all-encompassing. This was obvious in His relationship with everyone that He came into contact with. Despite the circumstances, or the consequences, His first thought was always for others, even when He was nailed to the cross.

Jesus commanded His followers to love one another as He loves us. This will inevitably include a degree of self-sacrifice. In our ministry of love to one another, we must show others the same compassion and forgiving love that the Lord has for us. Only in so doing, can the wounds of this world be healed. Harmony between people can only be achieved through obedience to Christ's commands. Then you, through His grace, can personally play an important role in the healing of society.

Holy Spirit of God, fill me with the desire and the ability to love my neighbor as You love me.

~ Amen ~

AUGUST 28

The decisive test of discipleship

"By this all men will know that you are my disciples, if you love one another." (Jn. 13:35)

Christ hands down many commands to His disciples. How we respond to these distinguishes us from those who do not acknowledge His sovereignty in their lives. The Christian's standards are the standards of Christ and, in his conduct and disposition, he strives to reflect the image of Christ.

Christian discipleship implies an honorable way of life and the doing of good deeds. It is impossible to live in intimate harmony with Christ without something of His loveliness being reflected in our lives. The Lord not only expects this difference, but the ungodly world expects it of you as well.

The litmus test of genuine discipleship is the love Christians have for one another. Good deeds without love lack the power of inspired discipleship, and faith degenerates into a series of good deeds that lack purpose.

Christ knows all our weaknesses and gives us the love we lack so that we can achieve His purpose in our lives. If we find it difficult to love, we need only open our lives to His Spirit, and allow Him to love others through us.

I ask that Your love will take possession of my life, O Lord, so that I will reflect the quality of Your love.

~ Amen ~

Messengers from Christ

AUGUST 29

"Peace be with you. As the Father has sent me, I am sending you." (Jn. 20:21)

Christians are called to a purposeful life. You are in the service of His Majesty, the living Christ, and you have voluntarily accepted the responsibility of serving Him. This means that you accept all the disciplines of a spiritual life, so that your love for Him can increase and so that you can be His efficient ambassador.

Where will you serve Jesus? For a privileged small number, their ministry will lead them to foreign countries and exciting circumstances, but for the majority of Christian believers it will mean service in the world around them. You may be in commerce or in a profession, hold a position of authority, or fill a humble post, you may be a homemaker; but wherever you are, you are called to be His representative. People who know about your loyalty to Him, will expect you to maintain certain standards in your speech and in your conduct.

If your life is filled with the love of Jesus Christ, your faith will bring a message of hope and love, wherever He uses you.

Here am I, Master, send me to serve You wherever You may need me.

~ Amen ~

August 30 — Be a comforter

They approach and come forward; each helps the other and says to his brother, "Be strong!" (Is. 41:5-6)

Life is not easy for the average person. The spiraling cost of living, stressful relationships, the fear of unemployment, the specter of ill-health, all contribute to make life difficult. Unfortunately, many people believe that disappointments and the misery that emerges from them cannot be avoided.

As a Christian, you are not guaranteed freedom from problems. If you bemoan your fate and feel that God has disappointed you, you become part of the mass choir that sings a song of woe about the afflictions and the unfairness of life.

If you have the Eternal Spirit of the living Christ in you, He will prevent you from sinking into the quicksand of depression and negativity. You will look for solutions to life's problems, and you will be content, in childlike faith, to cast all your cares upon Christ.

Because you know that through the power of Christ's spirit you can triumph over negative circumstances, you are able to comfort others. Then they, in turn, will be able to look past the temporary and the negative, and see the glorious future that God has planned for them.

Powerful Savior, let my faith be so positive that I will be able to assist others to overcome their despair.

~ Amen ~

Take time to pray

For none of us lives to himself alone. (Rom. 14:7)

People always find the time to do those things that they would like to do, but are quick to find excuses for not doing the things that they don't like doing. This attitude affects every aspect of our lives, including the spiritual.

You have probably occasionally said that you do not have the time to pray, and pointed to your hectic program. It would be beneficial to answer the question honestly, "How eager am I to make my prayer life more meaningful?" There is usually time for the newspaper, the TV, and just to relax.

If this is your experience, it would be sensible to ask yourself why you are making excuses. Why is your prayer life without splendor and power? Why has your faith become a burden instead of an inspiration of hope and faith? This happens when you no longer reach out to God in prayer, or if all your prayers have become expressions of your personal desires. True prayer broadens your spiritual and intellectual horizons and, at the same time, makes your relationship with your Savior and Redeemer more profound.

O Lord, my God, help me to develop a meaningful and powerful prayer life under the guidance of the Holy Spirit.

~ Amen ~

September

Heavenly Guide, I long to begin
this month with faith, hope,
and love in my heart.
I want to believe unconditionally:
like Abraham and Enoch and Moses
and all those in the gallery
of heroes in Hebrews 11.
But so often I am more like Thomas;
I first want to feel and see;
my faith is often limited to my senses.
I so want to believe the unseen and profess:
"My Lord and my God!" I want to experience
perfect hope, hope that all the ardent and noble
ideals of my heart will be realized;
that my spiritual life will grow
in knowledge, love and truth.
I want to love my neighbor with a sincere,
unselfish love that breaks down
the walls that divide us
Guide me into a true understanding
of faith and hope and love!

~ Amen ~

SEPTEMBER 1

Find encouragement in God

Open my eyes that I may see wonderful things in your law. (Ps. 119:18)

Despondency and discouragement are common in the world today. Emotions rise and fall as rapidly as mercury in a barometer, creating an unstable and insecure existence. The result is that many people are unhappy and not very sure of themselves. This negatively influences their actions, plans and decisions.

If you want to "live" rather than simply "exist" you should remain positive. If things are going well, enjoy life and stay positive. If things are not going well, then analyze your situation, identify the problem and deal with it.

You will need to have a faith that is strong to enable you to bear the afflictions, handle the problems, overcome the obstacles and eventually live triumphantly. Such a faith is developed through prayer, during which you seek the assistance of the living Christ. Constantly search the Scripture for examples of God's wondrous deeds. You will find one example after another where ordinary people were enabled to overcome great difficulties in the strength of the Lord. Find your encouragement in Jesus Christ and in His Word and you will triumph over depression.

Word that became flesh, I thank You for the future hope that You pour into my heart when I trust in You.

~ Amen ~

God is in control

Then Job replied to the Lord: "I know that you can do all things; no plan of yours can be thwarted." (Job 42:1)

Everywhere you go you will meet pessimists who find little or nothing that is right with this world. They see no hope for the future and they carry with them an atmosphere of gloom and dejection.

Rather than give in to despair, consider the greatness of God. Look back over the years and you will find many examples of the wonderful ways in which God transforms despair into lively hope; changes sorrow into joy and turns defeat into victory.

The one example that rises above all the others is the way in which God used the horror of Jesus' crucifixion to demonstrate the wonder of His forgiving love in the glory of the resurrection. Those of little faith believe Golgotha was the end of a sorrowful road, but Easter Sunday ushered in the beginning of a wonderful new life: God's plan for the redemption of mankind had been completed.

When things around you appear dark and terrifying, hold on to the promises of God. Remember the mighty deeds that He has performed, and continue in confidence and with the certain knowledge that He is wholly in control.

Almighty God and loving Father, my heart's knowledge that You are in control allows me to be courageous even in dark days. Guide me on Your path and keep my faith strong.

~ Amen ~

Grow in faith

Immediately the boy's father exclaimed, "I do believe; help me overcome my unbelief!" (Mk. 9:24)

Many Christians urge their fellow-believers to, "Just believe!" They assure them that wonderful things will happen if they do. But they don't tell them how such a faith can be obtained.

You believe in Jesus Christ for the common things in life, things that would have happened as a matter of course. But you need a faith that will work when storm clouds gather ominously around you.

Through the grace of God it isn't very difficult to develop a mature and sincere faith. Recall an incident in your life when something out of the ordinary happened. Look for something small to thank God for, an instance when you believed and God answered your prayer. It might not be something big or significant, but when you recall the incident, it strengthens your faith in a wonderful way. Suddenly you are able to say, "God was really at work in my life."

Make a habit of remembering small answers to prayer. Your faith will gradually grow to the extent where you will receive bigger revelations from God. Use the faith that you already have and you will grow in faith and grace.

Loving Master, I want to grow in my faith so that I can bring glory and honor to You in everything I do and say.

~ Amen ~

Love is the foundation of faith

Love always protects, always trusts, always hopes, always perseveres. (1 Cor. 13:7)

Love that always trusts concerns our relationship with God. Love takes God at His word and believes absolutely that I can make each of His promises my own, knowing that they are steadfast and true. This is a love born from the certainty that God exists.

It also concerns our relationships with others. This implies a love that is always willing to believe the best about others. If we act as though we do not trust people and regard them with suspicion, they will be unreliable. If we treat them in a way that shows we trust them completely, they will become reliable people through our loving trust.

We must protect our children with our love as we bring them to maturity. Even when they make mistakes, we must teach them that they can become responsible adults if they use their freedom correctly. Through our loving trust in them, it will become increasingly difficult for them to lie, swear or avoid their responsibilities. They will know that, through our faith in them, they will become stronger people and, in turn, it will be easier for them to believe.

Holy Father, help me to use my freedom with love to Your glory.

~ Amen ~

SEPTEMBER 5

We believe without seeing

Therefore we are always confident ... We live by faith, not by sight. (2 Cor. 5:6-7)

When you are battling with problems, difficulties or disappointments, or when you have to make important decisions, do you trust God sufficiently to place yourself and your future unconditionally in His hand; and are you sure that everything will work together for your good?

Jesus came to confirm that God loves you unconditionally. His care, help and compassion are unquestionable. You are precious in His sight. Remember that He died on Golgotha for your sake and in your place. Know then that Christ will not allow anything to harm you. With this assurance, you can trust God unconditionally in everything. Then you will walk along His paths, doing His will.

To ensure peace and tranquility of mind, place yourself, your plans and your problems in the hands of your Savior. Discuss your problems with Him in prayer. Remember you are talking to someone who, by grace, calls you His friend.

Then you will experience the living presence of Christ in every situation of life. He will guide you through His Spirit to where you experience peace and tranquility of mind. Even if you cannot see the complete road ahead, faith will carry you through.

Lord, be with me in the dark days, and shine the light of Your presence before me so that I do not stumble.

~ Amen ~

Your life is in loving hands

But I trust in you, O LORD; I say, "You are my God." My times are in your hands; deliver me from my enemies and from those who pursue me. (Ps. 31:14-15)

Some people can quickly sum up a situation and then act on it. Others need more time to consider the circumstances before they decide on any plan of action.

Some people are able to discern the spiritual truth straight away and to act on it immediately. Others gradually come to an understanding of the truth, but their reaction to it is no less sincere.

Your life is determined by God's perfect timing. If it is easy for you to discern God's will, then be careful that you don't move faster than God intended you to. If God's will for your life is discerned more gradually, then take care that it doesn't become an excuse for lethargy.

It is possible to be in perfect harmony with God's timing for your life. If you trust God unconditionally, there will be order in your life, instead of chaos. That is why it is so important to spend time with God in prayer. That is how the tempo of your life will come into perfect harmony with God's timing. And thus you will learn to really live.

Father, please fulfill my needs in Your perfect timing. Fill me with peace in Your presence that comes from trusting You.

~ Amen ~

Is your concept of God broad enough?

"How great is God – beyond our understanding!" (Job 36:26)

One obstacle to spiritual development is our limited concept of God. You believe that God loves and cares for you. You accept that He is all-powerful, all-knowing and omnipresent. But as soon as disaster threatens, you forget about God. You fail to draw on the wisdom, calmness and strength that He has placed at your disposal. Your problems appear to be bigger than your concept of God.

Broaden your vision of God while things are going well. Make more use of your quiet time with Him. Increase your awareness of the greatness of God and use the grace He gives you to get to know Him more intimately. When storms start looming you will find that you possess spiritual reserves that will enable you to be strong, no matter how difficult your circumstances are.

The greater your concept of God becomes, the more strength you will draw from Him. Your faith will become a true experience of God Himself. He will assure you of His presence at all times. Know how great your God is; you will possess solid faith!

Great and wonderful God, grant me a spirit of appreciation for Your greatness, so that my spirit and perspective may be broadened.

~ Amen ~

Your anchor in life

"There is no one holy like the Lord; there is no one besides you; there is no Rock like our God." (1 Sam. 2:2)

Every person needs reassurance and support sometimes. Even those who regard themselves as totally self-sufficient come to a point where their own resources are insufficient to meet the needs of the situation they find themselves in. Then they need something or someone to enable them to handle the situation.

Some people turn to professional counselors for advice; others go for medical assistance; yet others turn to their friends. There are even those who try to fight their way through the dilemma in their own strength. While all these methods can provide some help, they won't have the assurance that the problem won't recur, or that they will be able to handle it if it does.

The only sure and lasting solution comes from God. Never make the mistake of leaving God out. He cares for you in every situation. Because Christ is the same yesterday, today and forever, you can be assured of His constant presence in every situation. Other things can help you survive, but only God can give you abiding peace.

Savior, by putting my life in Your hands I know that all things will work together for my benefit because You love me.

~ Amen ~

Light in times of darkness

Even in darkness light dawns for the upright, for the gracious and compassionate and righteous man. (Ps. 112:4)

Every believer who wishes to know God more intimately, must accept that there will be times when dark clouds of affliction will cover his path. At first God is such a glorious reality to you, doubt doesn't have a chance to creep into your heart and joy floods your life. Unfortunately this condition is not permanent. Perhaps as a result of disobedience, or because your love for the Lord wanes, the cloud of despondency descends upon your spiritual life.

When that happens, it is essential to reestablish the truth that God is unchanging. His love for you remains exactly what it always was. He is still your Protector and Guide.

You may find the darkness hard to accept, and God may seem far off and uninvolved. Yet hold on steadfastly to the assurance that God loves you and that He cares for you. Never question His goodness or His purpose for your life. Fortunately, the dark times are also not permanent. You will step out of the shadows with new strength, and, being stronger and wiser, you will walk in His sunshine again.

I will trust You in the darkness, because I know that You are good.

~ Amen ~

The Christian's trust in God

SEPTEMBER 10

*But as for me, I watch in hope for the L*ORD*, I wait for God my Savior; my God will hear me.* (Mic. 7:7)

Some people believe that their lives and future are determined by the stars, others ask the guidance of fortune-tellers. These people come from all levels of society: the poor and the rich; the uneducated and the learned.

These methods, however trustworthy they may appear at face value, are not trustworthy enough to help us to handle the unknown. There is always the fear of uncertainty or failure, as well as the possibility that you will develop such an obsession with these things that, in the end, failure is all that you have left.

The only way in which you can be filled with self-confidence, is by believing in God. You will face problems, and when they arrive, doubt will certainly take hold of you sometimes. This is when Jesus comes to say to you, *"Take courage! It is I. Don't be afraid"* (Mt. 14:27). In their superstitious minds, the disciples thought that they had seen a ghost, but Christ brought them peace of mind. It is the selfsame peace that He wishes to bring to you and that He wants you to communicate to your fellowman.

Loving Savior, I place myself completely under Your control, for I know that You alone can guarantee me peace of mind.

~ Amen ~

SEPTEMBER 11

Do you truly believe?

"I do believe; help me overcome my unbelief!" (Mk. 9:24)

How solid is your faith? Have you reduced it to outward issues of attending church, singing songs of praise, listening to nice sermons and endeavoring to live a respectable life? Or do you believe that the dynamic and transforming omnipotence of a living God exists as the center of Christianity?

Your faith becomes reality when the external ceremonies of Christianity become a pulsating and powerful experience in your soul. When, through the power of Christ residing in you, you no longer see yourself as someone defeated by a secret, besetting sin. It starts the moment when you feel yourself to be in complete control of your own life, through God's Holy Spirit who resides in you and enables you to triumph over all sin.

You must develop the discipline to experience Christ's presence in your everyday life. Prayer, Bible study and fellowship with other believers are essential in the development of a spiritual maturity and the attainment of a positive, living and dynamic faith.

Lord, You are my only shelter. When I feel powerless and afraid, You will lead me through the darkness and give me renewed courage.

~ Amen ~

Equipped through faith

Though I have fallen, I will rise. Though I sit in darkness, the L ORD *will be my light.* (Mic. 7:8)

History shows that mankind has experienced dark times through the ages. There were times of economic depression; devastating wars; droughts, floods and famines; plagues and other dark dangers. And there are still places across the world where people live in fear and tension. They are surrounded by a dark cloud of despair and the future is a dark, unknown wasteland.

In order to survive in these circumstances it is extremely important to have a strong faith in the risen Christ. Dark times are the very times during which you can look back and see how God has always overcome the power of evil through His omnipotence and majesty. You will see how He always transforms defeat into victory; makes the weak strong; and transforms the darkness into radiant light.

Remind yourself of Golgotha. Nothing could have been more devastating than the death of Jesus Christ on the cross, and yet, there is nothing more triumphant than His resurrection from the dead. Put your faith and trust in God and you will step from the darkness of your despair into the glorious light of His love.

Lord Jesus, total trust in You means believing that You are always in control. Help me never to waver, but to put my hand in Yours.

~ Amen ~

The cornerstone of your faith

And now these three remain: faith, hope and love. But the greatest of these is love. (1 Cor. 13:13)

The Christian faith has many facets. Each person's tradition and personality influence his approach to Christ. Your spiritual life is weakened when you refuse to accept that another person's viewpoint could be correct even though it differs from yours.

The real test of your faith is the amount of love you have toward other believers, especially those whose viewpoint differs radically from yours. Such faith has its roots in a way of life that stays so close to Christ that His love flows through you to others. Your love for Christ includes loving all people who love Him, even though you may not agree with them on an intellectual level about matters such as dogma and church government.

Love is paramount in your spiritual life. There are times when it challenges and reprimands; it humbles you to lift you to great spiritual heights; it empties you of yourself, of covetousness and pride, to fill you with the love of God. That is why it increases your love for other people. If you love God and His love finds expression in you, you will love your fellow-believers as well.

Lord, I pray that love will flow through me and through all those who love You so that the world may know that we are Your disciples.

~ Amen ~

The light on your way

And God said: "Let there be light," and there was light. (Gen. 1:3)

SEPTEMBER 14

When we look back upon the road we have traveled, we tend to focus on things like adversity, violence, disasters and strife. When we then look toward the future everything seems gloomy, and we fear what will happen. The past has had its share of problems and so many people expect no better from the future. This makes them despondent.

You must think and believe positively in order to obtain positive results. As you travel through life, you will have to draw on the reserves of your faith. You must call into remembrance all the great deeds of God throughout the centuries and place your trust in Him to lead you on His perfect path.

The prayer of your heart every day should be, "Lead me, O Light of the world!" Jesus Christ is still the Light of the world and He has promised that those who follow Him will never walk in darkness. There is no darkness that He cannot illuminate. He invites you to continue your journey through life in His company. Take His hand in faith and trust and experience Him as the light of your life.

God of light and truth, thank You that Your Son has illuminated my life so that I can walk into the future in faith and trust. Be my light, even when darkness falls around me.

~ Amen ~

SEPTEMBER 15

"I know for certain!"

"Yet not my will, but yours be done." (Lk. 22:42)

Many disappointments come upon us unexpectedly, many ordeals cross our path in life. Often we cannot see the sense or meaning in them. Whether these are major troubles or minor irritations, we must confront and handle them all.

The Lord's love for us is endlessly tender and positive. He assures us, *"Never will I leave you; never will I forsake you"* (Heb. 13:5). He wants us to trust where we cannot see. A sincere faith says, "I know for certain that God's will is best for me." Faith leaves the choice up to God, with the words His Son taught us, "Your will be done!" Then we will experience His peace flowing through us and touching our innermost being, and we will radiate joy around us.

Our faithful prayer every day must simply be, "Your will be done!" This is the only way in which we can get to know His peace here on earth. We must trust in Him through grace, until we meet Him face to face. His perfect will functions always for our own good and to our benefit, even though it does not immediately appear so.

Eternal God and Father, thank You for sending Your Son to come and teach me what it means to let Your will be done in my life. Let Your Spirit assist me in this.

~ Amen ~

Your shield and your stronghold

The Lord is my rock, my fortress and my deliverer; my God is my rock, in whom I take refuge. He is my shield and the horn of my salvation, my stronghold.
(Ps. 18:2)

Regardless of who you are, there are bound to be times when you need someone you can fully trust. You might need advice, assistance or encouragement and you look for someone you can trust to assist you. But people are often fickle and untrustworthy. Sometimes those you approach for help are so engrossed in their own problems that they have very little time to assist you.

The joy of Christianity is the fact that God is only a prayer away. Whatever your problem or need, whenever it may occur, the Lord is waiting for you to turn to Him. Submit your problems to Him as He accompanies you on the way He has set out for your life. He is omniscient, omnipotent and all-seeing, therefore you can rest assured that His way will be to your benefit.

The absolute trustworthiness of the risen Christ, who is the same yesterday, today and forevermore, is your guarantee that God's way is the best for you. Therefore, when you are in need, turn to Him and allow Christ to enfold you with His love and to protect and encourage you.

Lord, with the psalmist I confess that You are the strength and the stronghold of my life.

~ Amen ~

Plan with God

SEPTEMBER 17

So that your faith might not rest on men's wisdom, but on God's power. (1 Cor. 2:5)

Have you, or your loved ones, ever experienced the disappointment of unfulfilled dreams, watched carefully planned dreams disintegrate and hope collapse like a house of cards? Many people who experience such a set-back never recover. They are unwilling to risk another disaster, and so a tremendous amount of potential lies wasted and unused.

Some mock the idea that you need to call for God's help to fulfill your plans. They promote self-sufficiency in everything they undertake and trust completely in their own ability. That is why, when success is achieved, they also take all the praise for themselves. But if their plans do not succeed, they experience the destructive results of failure.

When you trust God in everything you do, and submit to His will and obey Him, you might feel that things move too slowly for you. Be patient and steadfastly put your trust in God. Then you will have peace of mind, knowing that God is in control and that the fulfillment of your plans will be to your lasting benefit. Trust God's protective love when you make plans for your life.

Lord, I know that when I bring my plans for my life to You, You will show me what Your plans are, and help me to succeed in all things.

~ Amen ~

God remains in control

He is before all things, and in him all things hold together. (Col. 1:17)

There are times when it seems as though everything is going wrong. The present is unstable and the future is uncertain. Regardless of what problems might be upsetting your personal life or the world around you, look back over history. You will discover that nations and individuals have struggled through disasters, hardships and dangers. People were confronted with sorrow and adversity, just as we are confronted today by situations that cause us to struggle.

Before becoming despondent, acknowledge the greatness, glory and constancy of God. He called the world into existence, He created man, He has kept vigil over His creation and cared for us through the ages and sheltered us in every disaster. He is the Creator God who will never abandon His workmanship. In His great love, He gave His Son to the world, so that whoever believes in Him shall not perish but have everlasting life (see Jn. 3:16). Hold on to His promises; place your entire trust and faith in the living Christ. Through Him you will survive all dangers and adversity.

You are eternal, Lord, and the workmanship of Your creation bears testimony to Your great glory.
~ Amen ~

Blessed assurance

Commit to the Lord whatever you do, and your plans will succeed. (Prov. 16:3)

Planning is important in every area of life. You plan for the future, for your marriage, for your finances and for retirement. It would be interesting to calculate how much time and energy are wasted on useless planning.

There is, however, a way to ensure that your planning will be successful. It requires strict spiritual discipline to make it effective and it must be undertaken with sincerity and honesty. It requires solid faith and trust in God and in His promises.

Whatever your concern may be, lay it before God in prayer, trusting in Him completely. Talk to Him, submit all the details to Him, tell Him about your expectations and fears, seek His all-wise guidance and ask Him for clarity and the gift of discernment and wisdom, to know and to understand when He gives you the answer.

Then trust Him steadfastly, leaving the matter in His hands. In His own perfect time and way, He will show you how to bring it to pass. And when He does, move ahead obediently and gratefully, remembering that He is with you every step of the way.

Dear Lord, guide me to follow Your commands and to fulfill Your will in obedience.

~ Amen ~

The kingdom and the power and the glory!

The LORD has established his throne in heaven, and his kingdom rules over all. (Ps. 103:19.)

In a world where it would seem that evil reigns over truth and justice, we must never lose sight of the fact that power, sovereignty, and majesty reside in God. It is this knowledge that encourages and strengthens us even in our darkest hour.

History attests to many instances where it appeared as if everything was lost: when anarchy and lawlessness threatened to destroy all order; when selfishness and lust dominated; when powerful nations attempted to destroy weak ones; when innocent people were oppressed and tortured.

Despite all these things, truth and justice eventually triumphed. For a time anxiety, concern, fear and suffering were rife, but ultimately the power of evil was destroyed and the righteous prevailed.

However hopeless circumstances seem, God is almighty and He is still in control. Place your trust in Jesus Christ your Redeemer and find encouragement and peace in the knowledge that our setbacks are merely temporary, because Christ has already conquered the world (see Jn. 16:33).

Almighty God, great wonders are performed by Your hand and Your mighty deeds are seen in the history of mankind. For ever and ever You are God!

~ Amen ~

SEPTEMBER 21

Establish trust through partnership

So we say with confidence, "The Lord is my helper; I will not be afraid. What can man do to me?" (Heb. 13:6)

If you try to tackle life's difficulties and problems in your own strength and wisdom, you will likely fight a losing battle. You might not constantly grumble or complain, but if you were honest with yourself, you would have to admit that there are moments when you long for your burden to be lifted.

It is advisable to become quiet before God, and to remember that He is closer to you than your own breath. Do not take God's help for granted. When you seek His help, place what you are and what you have at His disposal. Become God's partner in your daily life. This partnership means that you should constantly carry out the will of your heavenly Partner, and do it in such a devoted and enthusiastic way that fear will have no place in your life.

When you have conquered fear through working together with God, you can face everything with a peaceful confidence that is the direct consequence of your union with God. Because God is your Helper, and because you serve Him joyfully, you can step fearlessly and confidently into the future.

Good Shepherd, because You are my Helper and I serve You with sincerity, my life is filled with trust that is born from my relationship with You.

~ Amen ~

Attempt great things

He is your praise; he is your God, who performed for you those great and awesome wonders. (Deut. 10:21)

Many people adapt their lives according to what others think of them. They disappear among the masses and lose their identity. At times, however, they become aware of stirrings in their spirit. This is because they have the seeds of eternity in them.

Those who become aware of this start searching for broader horizons of spiritual and mental experiences. They become dissatisfied with their present situation and yearn to expand their future. But the ordinary, unfulfilling life they lead seems to restrict their search. They long to move ahead with new insights, but are constantly held back by certain influences. Many fear that they will never be able to escape from the past and regress into their old life, with crumbled hopes and shattered dreams.

If God has given you a vision or a mission, then you can be sure it will require effort and hard work. God guides individuals by entrusting them with tasks which seem to be above their ability. Only if you accept the challenge and trust God, will you be able to find out what you are capable of.

My Lord, I pray that I would not be satisfied with what others say about me, but that I will seek and find Your purpose for my life, and trust You to bring it to completion.

~ Amen ~

SEPTEMBER 23

You are God's child!

How great is the love the Father has lavished on us, that we should be called children of God! And that is what we are! The reason the world does not know us is that it did not know him. (1 Jn. 3:1)

If the truth of this Scripture becomes a personal reality, transformation occurs that brings meaning and glory to your daily life. Perhaps you approach the future with a lack of confidence and you are unsure about the decisions you make. Let your faith in Jesus Christ transform this negative attitude into a positive approach to life. By grace, God is now your Father, and because you love and obey Him, you can make your life what He intended it to be.

As the Lord's will is revealed through your life, a very intimate and strong bond will develop between you and Him. You will have the glorious assurance that He is truly your Father and that you are irrevocably His child. This intimate relationship makes it so much easier to be obedient to the heavenly Father.

Strengthen these close ties with your Father by commitment and obedience. Thus the grace of God is established in your life every day, to His glory and honor and to your immeasurable benefit and joy.

Thank You, Lord Jesus, for the joy of Your salvation that has transformed my life.

~ Amen ~

What God can accomplish through you

"Remain in me, and I will remain in you. No branch can bear fruit by itself; it must remain in the vine. Neither can you bear fruit unless you remain in me." (Jn. 15:4)

We worship a God who performs miracles. You can confidently call on Him in times of stress and tension. Experience has proved that He will answer in the way He sees best. He will always give you what you need because He is the Giver of every perfect gift and you are the blessed receiver.

Discovering God's will for your life can be an exciting adventure. You may try out various directions before you finally discover the path upon which He wishes to lead you. But when you possess the inner conviction that you are within His holy will, you will discover that you are no longer working for Him, but that He is working through you.

When this happens the road ahead opens up miraculously. Problems become opportunities and your faith becomes practical, alive and dynamic. You realize that by working with God you become His effective instrument. You will never discover your full potential in the service of Christ until you realize what God can accomplish through you.

Holy Father, help me through Your guidance to become an instrument in Your hand so that I may work within Your will and to Your glory.

~ Amen ~

The voice of God

SEPTEMBER 25

"Go and lie down, and if he calls you, say, 'Speak, Lord, for your servant is listening.'" (1 Sam. 3:9)

A careful study of Scripture reveals many occasions when people heard the voice of God. We, today, do not experience such dramatic moments. However, it does not mean that God is no longer talking to us. There are numerous instances when God undoubtedly touched people, radically changing their lives. As they obeyed, God led them in a specific direction.

If you walk close to God and remain sensitive to the whisperings of the Holy Spirit, you will soon be in harmony with His will. This requires the discipline of prayer and meditation. Learn to be silent in the holy presence of the Lord. You will gradually become more and more aware of His voice in all situations of your life.

Then, instead of acting on impulse, you learn to wait for the Lord and for His guidance. It may be revealed to you through intuition, by the circumstances in which you find yourself, or through the guidance and actions of those around you. But you will know without a doubt when God speaks to you. God speaks to us in a thousand voices, if our hearts would only listen.

Lord, You are so wonderful, because You cleansed me with Your blood. Thank You that I can live as a redeemed person.

~ Amen ~

Extract the most from your faith

"Whoever has will be given more ... Whoever does not have, even what he has will be taken from him." (Mt. 13:12)

A dedicated Christian must also be a Word-based Christian. Refusal to use the Scriptures to inform your moral conduct may cause your faith to become emotionally unbalanced. And then the message of the gospel becomes distorted to suit your own personal conviction and ideology. Eventually all the power of faith disappears in wishful thinking and unscriptural didactics.

The church and the world have a serious need for disciplined Christianity that affirms the teachings of Jesus. The one truth that embraces all others is, *"As I have loved you, so you must love one another"* (Jn. 13:34).

The discipline required to live a life of Christian love demands a strength that can only be acquired from the Holy Spirit. This discipline is kept alive through prayer and contemplation and a constant yearning for a more profound experience with God.

I plead with You, O living Jesus, for the gift of Your Holy Spirit so that I can experience my faith to its fullest potential.

~ Amen ~

To identify with Christ

SEPTEMBER 27

"The life I live in the body, I live by faith in the Son of God, who loved me and gave himself for me." (Gal. 2:20)

This is one of the most inspiring, yet challenging texts in the New Testament. Love, peace, strength and other attributes of Christ become a glorious reality to all who accept Him and are obedient to Him.

No human being can, in his own strength, achieve an intimate relationship with the living Christ. It is only through God's goodness and grace that we can experience the reality of Christ's Spirit. Identifying with Christ means that we learn to walk as closely to Him as is possible.

In order to be one with Christ implies carrying His message of redemption to the world. It means experiencing some of the pain that He suffered as a result of the depravity of mankind. It means to be compassionate and generous, to love others in His Spirit and with His love.

To identify with Christ you need to surrender and commit yourself completely to Him. Your attitudes, behavior, motives and lifestyle should be the expression of the Spirit of Christ in you. Identification with Christ means to become more and more like the Master.

Thank You, heavenly Teacher, that I may grow in the grace and wisdom of my Redeemer, Jesus Christ. For this I thank and praise You.

~ Amen ~

A faith that counts

The only thing that counts is faith expressing itself through love. (Gal. 5:6)

Different people have different views on what is most important in our spiritual lives. Some people stick meticulously to a set of rules, and often their love is limited to those people who agree with them in every detail.

Your faith will be insufficient and ineffective if it does not lead you to a more profound knowledge and awareness of God. An intimate relationship with Jesus Christ leads to such a sincere love that His presence becomes a living reality for you. An active faith in the resurrected and exalted Savior forms the basis of all Christian doctrine.

Faith is alive and meaningful when it is expressed through love. Without love, faith becomes bigoted and the height, depth and eternal nature of God's love cannot be experienced. If our love is to be acceptable to God, as well as function properly, it has to be inspired and confirmed by His perfect love.

If you possess a living faith manifested in love, you have the basic qualities of a practical, inspired and effective religion that is acceptable to God.

Lord, Your Word teaches me to love You with my whole heart, soul and mind, and to love my neighbor as myself. Grant me the strength to abide by these commandments.

~ Amen ~

Stand by your convictions

Simon Peter answered, "You are the Christ, the Son of the living God." (Mt. 16:16)

SEPTEMBER 29

Many people long for a stronger faith. They attend services and are active in church affairs; but their spiritual life has become lukewarm and their relationship with Christ humdrum.

All of us need to answer the question that Jesus put to Simon Peter, "What about you? Who do you say I am?" This question may be put to us when we do not know who to turn to for help or what we must do; it might loom before us when we are frustrated and dissatisfied with our own seemingly empty and aimless spiritual life.

To benefit fully from Christian experience, and to know the fullness and abundance of true life that Jesus offers us, you must have a personal knowledge of the living Christ. This does not only mean learning everything about Him that there is to learn; it means knowing Him personally and surrendering to Him. Acknowledge Christ's sovereignty and then abundant life will be yours. That is why Jesus came to this world.

Make me Your prisoner, O Lord, because only then will I be truly free.

~ Amen ~

Fly with the wings of an eagle

"But those who hope in the Lord shall renew their strength. They will soar on wings like eagles." (Is. 40:31)

We get burdened by so much pettiness in life. Some issues are of little importance, but others are molehills that became mountains. We so easily get bogged down by things that don't really matter. The vision of what you can be is easily dimmed by a narrow-minded view and petty spirit.

Christians can rise above irritations by trusting in the Lord under all circumstances and remaining conscious of His living presence. It is impossible to be petty and narrow-minded when the love of Christ fills your heart and mind. Loving others by the power of the Holy Spirit means rising above pettiness and reaching heights that the God of love desires all His children to live at.

Do not allow circumstances to claim so much of your attention that you lose sight of spiritual realities. These are the very things that add depth, purpose and meaning, goal and direction to your existence. By developing a consciousness of the presence of the living God and by always trusting in Him, you will be enabled to fly like the eagle, and see things in their right perspective.

Holy Spirit, fill me with the love of the Father and of the Son and of the Spirit so that I can love others with Your love and so demonstrate my faith in You.

~ Amen ~

October

Lord God,
You endured suffering for the sake
of the world, and also for me.
All your suffering and indignity,
all Your sorrow and pain;
every word spoken on the cross –
even those when You were forsaken by God –
was on my behalf. Lord Jesus, You gave
Your life for me even though
I am not worthy of that sacrifice.
In profound gratitude I dedicate myself
anew to You: body, soul, and spirit.
Guide me through this month,
make me Your faithful disciple
and a fearless witness of Your love.
Through the cross, let me realize
the wretchedness of my sin,
so that I will flee from it to Your grace.
Through the cross, let me see Your love
so that I may take refuge in You.
For Your love's sake.

~ Amen ~

OCTOBER 1

Jesus, the source of all true happiness

"Hosanna! Blessed is he who comes in the name of the Lord! Blessed is the coming kingdom of our father David!" (Mk. 11:9-10)

Jesus is the source of all true happiness and blessing. To be blessed, we must know Jesus as our personal Savior and Redeemer; we must commit our lives to Him; we must be obedient to His will under all circumstances.

We all search for happiness but we want to determine what it should consist of. Then we run the risk of missing Christ's blessing. Our "man-made" happiness often depends upon "luck": a sudden and unexpected change in our condition. And the focus becomes materialistic and self-centered.

Human happiness is something that life can offer, and then, just as suddenly, take away again. Man, in his short-sightedness, calls it "happiness" when things go his way for a while. But happiness in God is centered in Christ and His will for our lives. It is an eternal blessing that depends on our relationship with Him.

Lord Jesus, I praise Your glorious Name, for You are the source of all my happiness. You delivered me from sin and made me a child of God.

~ Amen ~

Rejoice in the Lord!

Then the people of Israel – the priests, the Levites and the rest of the exiles – celebrated the dedication of the house of God with joy. (Ezra 6:16)

Sadly, there are many people who see Christianity as cheerless and something to be done out of fear. They attend church services out of a false sense of duty and habit. Such an attitude tragically deprives them of the greatest of all joys: joy in the Lord.

God offers you fullness of life. Turn to Him and you will become more aware of His life-giving Spirit. Goals which seemed unattainable are suddenly within your reach; adversity does not overwhelm you because in Him you find the strength to overcome it; a newly found confidence replaces your feelings of failure. Day by day your faith grows stronger.

As you open yourself to the Holy Spirit, you will find that your worship, Bible study and prayer life gain new meaning. If you place your trust in the living Christ, you will discover that God is no longer a remote being, but an integral part of your life. Worship ought to be a joyful experience. Open yourself to the Holy Spirit, and He will raise you from despondency to ecstasy in Christ.

O Holy Spirit, come into my life and fill me with the joy of the Lord.

~ Amen ~

OCTOBER 3

Gratitude

Always giving thanks to God the Father for everything, in the name of our Lord Jesus Christ. (Eph. 5:20)

Many Christians find life so hard and demanding. Wherever they turn they experience opposition and discouragement. Their human relations seem to be in a mess. Nothing they attempt seems to work out to their satisfaction.

Unfortunately many Christians have lost the art of being thankful. They are so overwhelmed by setbacks and problems that a cloud of depression has descended upon them and they find very little to thank God for.

When Christians stop giving thanks, they lose a source of great inspiration and spiritual strength. First and foremost you must thank God that He loves you and cares for you. Just thinking about the compassionate love God has for you should inspire you to be sincerely grateful.

Being thankful is a powerful factor in your spiritual life. It dispels the dark clouds of depression and despondency. The only way to establish the power of thanksgiving is to practice it every day. Start every day with a sincere prayer of appreciation to your heavenly Father for the gift of life. Then you will find the key to a victorious and abundant life.

Holy Lord Jesus, I praise You because You have given me the power to overcome darkness and despair.

~ Amen ~

Why should we praise and glorify God?

OCTOBER 4

Praise, O servants of the LORD, praise the name of the LORD. Let the name of the LORD be praised, both now and forevermore. (Ps. 113:1-2)

Why should God be praised and glorified? Why should we tell Him how almighty, all-knowing and omnipresent He is? Because He asks us to. God never asks us to do things that are meaningless and ritualistic. Praising and glorifying God is more than simply listing His divine attributes.

The complexity of the human temperament compels it to reach out to something higher and greater than itself. This yearning can be fulfilled by praising and glorifying God. Praise connects us to the one who knows and understands the desires of our hearts. God can manage fine without our praise, but we cannot manage without the strength and inspiration that comes from our praise of Him.

True praise is one of the greatest inspirational forces in life. It raises you up from your spiritual despondency and enables you to live in communion with your heavenly Father. Praise brings you into the holy presence of God.

Holy Father, I enter Your gates with adulation, with praise I go into Your temple court. I enter into Your presence with joy and thanksgiving.

~ Amen ~

Be grateful for what you have

"When they received it (the money), they began to grumble against the landowner." (Mt. 20:11)

Why do so many people waste time and energy on insignificant and unimportant things? When people are united by incessant complaining, they harm themselves and make no positive contribution to the community to which they belong.

You do not have to look very far to find something to complain about, if you really want to. But a wise person tries to restore the balance by thinking about something for which he can be grateful. Remember, for everything that causes grievance, there is something for which you can be eternally grateful.

If you have developed a grateful heart, you have discovered one of the great secrets of life. Try to find something that you can be grateful for and praise God for it. Then incorporate the thought into your way of life, so that your attitude becomes one of praise to God. Look for the way He helps and guides you in every sphere of your life. Then the powers of good will be revealed through you, and you will feel wonder and satisfaction at the ways of God.

I sometimes complain about such trivialities. Jesus, You endured Your suffering in silence so that I may be free. Please cleanse my heart and purify me.

~ Amen ~

Be continually grateful

Continue to live in him, rooted and built up in him, strengthened in the faith as you were taught, and overflowing with thankfulness. (Col. 2:6-7)

Many people restlessly pursue empty dreams of a better world and a better life. And then they become dissatisfied with life and develop a purposeless lifestyle that finds fault with everything. They focus so much on the flaws and faults around them that they fail to see the wonders of God and His grace.

Every detail of your life, from the cradle to the grave, is known to God. In His eternal design He plans what is best for you. Sometimes things go wrong, but God can change your situation so that light radiates from the darkness and hope is born from despair.

If you feel dejected, think back on all the good things that have happened in your life. Recall those times when you were conscious of Christ's presence and His love filled your heart.

Thank the Lord for His grace and blessings. Then the Holy Spirit will bring healing to your life and you will be filled with joy. Praise and gratitude lift your heart and honor God who is the giver of all that is good.

We praise and thank You, O Lord, with our hearts, our mouths and our hands, for all the wonders that You have done.

~ Amen ~

The blessing of gratitude

Always give thanks to God the Father for everything, in the name of our Lord Jesus Christ. (Eph. 5:20)

In the hustle and bustle of everyday life, it is so easy to forget about ordinary courtesy. People do nice things for us; shop assistants serve us with courtesy and a smile. But we forget that a word of appreciation could change their duty into a blessing.

The habit of saying "Thank you" enriches every aspect of our lives. It costs nothing, but creates joy for all concerned. If you doubt this, look out for times when courtesy and friendliness are shown toward you. Do you accept it as a matter of course or does it give your heart a lift?

If you were always ready to express thanks, you would discover how much joy you can bring to others. And your own life will be enriched too.

If this is true on an ordinary human level, how much more effective would it be if we were to express gratitude towards our Heavenly Father. All that we have, He gave to us, and we so seldom say thank You. When we do, our spirit is set free and we experience a joy and blessing that could only come from God.

Give me a grateful heart, O God, for all the wondrous things that You have done for us, but above all, for the sacrifice of Jesus, our Savior.

~ Amen ~

Start your day giving thanks

Rooted and built up in him, strengthened in the faith as you were taught, and overflowing with thankfulness. (Col. 2:7)

It is important that we, as children of God, maintain a positive and constructive attitude toward life. Insufficient rest can make you so irritable that you develop a wrong idea of what your life can and should be. Poor health can make you difficult to live with. Yet numerous invalids are channels of blessing for those who take care of them.

A healthy approach and positive attitude towards life does not come easily to the average person. We are subject to the whims of our emotions.

When you wake up in the morning your first responsibility is to take positive control of your thoughts and to thank God for the privilege of a new day. Recall some of the blessings that you tend to take for granted: your home, your friends and loved ones, your job and many more things.

Gratitude brings your heart into harmony with your heavenly Father. Then every day will be filled with true joy in the Lord. It requires an act of your will to start every day with true thanksgiving – but the benefits are worthwhile.

I want to start my day by thanking You for all the things I so often take for granted: for friends and family, for health and food, for this new day.

~ Amen ~

God's great gift

OCTOBER 9

May the grace of the Lord Jesus Christ, and the love of God, and the fellowship of the Holy Spirit be with you all. (2 Cor. 13:14)

When we reflect on the sacrifice God made through Jesus Christ on Golgotha for our redemption and salvation; the undying hope that He gave us through His triumphant resurrection from the dead; His power through the Holy Spirit, we cannot but be filled with wonder and respond with joy and praise? Our merciful Lord, Master and Friend so loved us that He freely gave these gifts to undeserving people like you and me.

There is no way that we can justly repay the Lord for His immeasurable love. However, we can, and should, open our lives to Him so that we can show His love to others. Christ commanded us to love one another as we love ourselves, and as He loves us.

Through the love of God and the grace of Jesus Christ, the Holy Spirit enables us to spread His love to everyone we come into contact with (see Acts 1:8).

Lord, I want to glorify You as my Father. Guide me so that I may be obedient to You in everything I do.

~ Amen ~

Work satisfaction

So I saw that there is nothing better for a man than to enjoy his work, because that is his lot. (Ecc. 3:22)

People often find their work monotonous because the initial fascination wears off and frustration and boredom set in.

God expects you to diligently use the special talents and aptitudes that He has woven into your life. No matter how elementary or routine some of the tasks you are required to perform are, He expects you to do your part with due care. You have an important contribution to make to the overall success of each project. Surgeons could not be successful if the theater staff were not efficient and conscientious. Even those whose job it is to clean the operating theater contribute to the eventual success of every operation. World class pianists would not be successful if the piano tuner did not apply himself to his work.

Whatever task you are called upon to perform, thank God that He has chosen you to do it. Commit everything you do to Him and you will find perfect joy in the knowledge that you are doing it well because you are doing it to the glory of your Master.

Help us, Lord, to glorify Your Name in everything we do. Help us always to recognize Your hand in our lives.

~ Amen ~

The unseen things are important

So we fix our eyes not on what is seen, but on what is unseen. For what is seen is temporary, but what is unseen is eternal. (2 Cor. 4:18)

Many people cannot appreciate the beauty of life because of their narrow spiritual perspective. However, a life that has been molded by the love and holiness of the Holy Spirit will reflect the glory of God and enjoy life in all its fullness.

When your thoughts are focused on Christ and you live for His glory, your spirit will be raised above time and place and you develop a greater understanding of eternal truths. You appreciate love, honor, purity, unselfishness and all that is noble in life, in spite of the rigors and realities of life in this world.

As your appreciation for the intrinsic beauty of life increases, you develop the ability to distinguish between that which is genuine and that which is feigned; between the wheat and the chaff. And then you realize that the things that you cannot see or touch are actually the most important things. He who claims only to believe in what he can see, touch and understand, has a very limited perspective on life, because the great wealth of God does not fall into any of these categories.

Beloved Lord, help me always to have a deep appreciation for the value of the spiritual realities that surround me.

~ Amen ~

Remember God's share in your success

But by the grace of God I am what I am, and his grace to me was not without effect. (1 Cor. 15:10)

Many people declare that they are "self-made" and they are rather satisfied with the product. If they think about the success that they have achieved in their careers, they claim all credit for themselves and look back on their achievements with self-satisfaction.

But it is foolish to believe that the honor for what has been achieved in life is yours alone. If God's hand of grace had not shielded you, if He had not granted you good health and a clear mind, you would not have triumphed over problems and adversities. Your success can, therefore, largely be attributed to the grace and guidance of God, whether or not you were always aware of it.

To lead a fulfilled and successful life you must be completly dependent on the living Christ. By acknowledging God's help in your achievements and by thanking Him for His grace and goodness, your life will be enriched. You will be filled with joy and happiness, knowing that the living God is involved in your success.

You bless us so undeservedly Lord, and more than we can ever expect. You are our salvation and courage for each day. Thank You for blessing us so abundantly.

~ Amen ~

Prayer and Praise

Is any one of you in trouble? He should pray. Is anyone happy? Let him sing songs of praise. (Jas. 5:13)

When a need arises in your life, you may require the service of an expert. Or you could go to a trusted friend for help or advice. Whoever you approach, you go to that person with the expectation that he will be able to help you. Regardless of the outcome, you will be grateful for the assistance that has been given you. And you usually express that gratitude with heartfelt thanks.

When you experience a crisis in your life, do not, in your confusion and anxiety, forget to take your problem to Jesus. He invites you to come to Him when you are tired and heavy-laden. Seek Christ's comfort, advice and protection. He cares for you and understands your needs. Bring your problems before Him in prayer and supplication and you will experience the peace of God in your heart.

But don't just leave things there. Thank God for the blessed assurance that He cares for you and that His hand will guide you through the maze of problems in your life. He leads you from the darkness into His marvelous light and love.

I want to praise You because You have promised that You will never leave me nor forsake me.

~ Amen ~

Appreciate your life

I will sacrifice a thank offering to you and call on the name of the Lord. (Ps. 116:17)

Sometimes when enthusiasm wanes and life loses its vibrancy. Such an unfortunate situation can arise quite unexpectedly.

To really appreciate life, keep your enthusiasm constantly alive. The gift of life must never be taken for granted, or it becomes common and boring and you lose your sense of anticipation and vision for the future. Take time to enjoy and appreciate the beauty of life.

Do you take the love and support of your family for granted? Can you still marvel at the sunrise? Have you become so blasé about all the suffering around you that it no longer moves you with compassion?

Your daily existence can so easily degenerate into drudgery, like a donkey that walks in a never-ending circle around a watermill. If you practice the art of appreciation, you can change your life into a beautiful and exciting adventure. If God becomes the center of your life and thoughts, you will discover that as you appreciate life, you will continuously be moving closer to Him, the Source of all real life.

Father, I appreciate all the beauty and wonder that fills my life day by day. Through praise, You keep my heart sensitive to the needs of others.

~ Amen ~

Fight depression

"Create in me a pure heart, O God, and renew a steadfast spirit within me." (Ps. 51:10)

When you feel depressed and life has lost its sparkle; when the future seems bleak, you probably find it hard to believe in God's compassion and love.

Stand still in the barrenness of your spiritual wilderness and look into the treasury of your memories. Recall those happy times when God guided you along difficult paths and touched your sorrow with His comfort. Remember when your whole life seemed to be falling apart and He upheld you with His loving hand. Start thanking Him for all these times.

Perhaps you spend too much time in the valley of despair and have sunk into self-pity. You have focused on your defeats and failures, and the mournful shadow of "what could have been" overshadows your mind. Begin to thank and praise God for His help in the past and His grace in the present. It is wonderful how praise and thanksgiving can change a contrite and depressed spirit. In His goodness, He will lift you out of the dark pit of despair!

I want to thank You for those times in my past when You have moved in my life, even though I was not aware of it at the time. You have always been near me to help me and encourage me.

~ Amen ~

What do we owe one another?

Let no debt remain outstanding, except the continuing debt to love one another. (Rom. 13:8)

We have so many reasons to give thanks to the Lord. Even when things go wrong, we must remember that God's mercy and love for us are infinite. His blessings are numerous. He granted you life and the freedom of choice to use it as you wish. You may be blessed with a happy family who loves you deeply. Even the most dejected person will, if he gives the topic careful consideration, find something for which he can thank and praise God.

How do you show God your gratitude for the bountiful grace in your life? Nothing you give or do can sufficiently pay for the love that He so lavishly pours on us. He showers us with blessings, and sacrificed His life for us.

Love can never be repaid sufficiently, because it is both precious and priceless. You cannot measure the magnitude of it. We can simply share it with others.

This is the best way to thank God for the great love that He has for you: share it with each person whose path crosses yours in life.

O Holy Spirit, help me to understand the lesson of true love as God has taught it to us through Jesus Christ. Grant that my every thought, word and deed will be an act of love for You.

~ Amen ~

Count your blessings

Whoever invokes a blessing in the land will do so by the God of truth. (Is. 65:16)

The person who has developed the habit of counting his blessings, is extremely happy. He knows that there is a solution for every problem and won't rest until he has found it. In the darkest moments he maintains a spirit of hope and optimism because he knows things will work out well.

To the optimist the simple things in life are a constant source of joy – the gift of spontaneous laughter, the sympathy and understanding of a loved one, the bright rays of the sun.

The more you count your blessings, the more it will seem as if God pours them upon your life. Your heart will overflow with gratitude for God's amazing love. When life becomes a burden to you and it feels as though you are living under an ominously dark sky, recalling your blessings is a sure way to keep a healthy perspective. Take note of God's abundant blessings in your life, appreciate them and thank Him for each one.

Father, how will I be able to express my gratitude in words? You bless me with so many things that were I to start listing them one by one, I would need eternity to thank You for each one.

~ Amen ~

The power of thanksgiving

To proclaim the year of the LORD's favor and the day of vengeance of our God, to comfort all who mourn ... They will be called oaks of righteousness, a planting of the LORD for the display of his splendor. (Is. 61:2-3)

Praise and thanksgiving have the power to change lives. Yet there are many committed disciples of the Lord who believe that we should only praise when our emotions run high and when everything goes well.

When the storm-clouds of life obscure the sunshine of God's love; when doubt threatens to destroy our faith in the goodness of God; when life seems to be falling apart – then, more than ever, it is necessary to offer praise and thanksgiving from the depths of our hearts.

You might ask how you can thank and praise God if it seems there is nothing to thank Him for. No mater what is happening in your life, remember that you are God's child. He loves you with a very special love and cares for you very much. He is still with you, even if you are not aware of His presense. Thank God that He is greater than any problem you may struggle with. As you focus on His greatness your life will rise above all destructive influences.

O Lord, teach me to rejoice in spite of the things that happen to me that seem to be so bad. Help me to remember that all things work together for my good because I love You.

~ Amen ~

Think and thank!

"I thank my God every time I remember you." (Phil. 1:3)

When life's path becomes steep and dark clouds ominously threaten to block out all inspiration, pause a while and consider how God has brought you along thus far. Remember all His abundant blessings.

There were probably moments when you thought that you would break under the strain, but God unexpectedly sent someone to bring you new hope and strength. At times disaster loomed and you felt that everything was lost, but God helped you rise from the ashes of failure.

The key that unlocks the door to a creative life is gratitude. In everything in life, look for something to be grateful for. Thank God for the good people He brings into your life, for doors He opened for you, for the wonder of friendship and, above all else, for the assurance of His eternal presence at all times.

When you assimilate this truth into your heart, you will approach the future with God-given confidence and the assurance that in the Name of Christ and in His strength, you can triumph in every situation.

Beloved Lord, I recall the blessings of the past and the joys of the present. Thank You for showers of blessings.

~ Amen ~

The blessings of a grateful heart

He who sacrifices thank offerings honors me. (Ps. 50:23)

The world is full of people who complain incessantly. Even though their complaints might be valid, such an attitude and can very quickly become a life pattern. Soon you forget that there are many more things to be grateful for than to complain about.

Nurture a spirit of appreciation and your quality of life will improve. Looking for things to be grateful for makes it easier to get on with others. It deepens your enjoyment of life and sheds happiness wherever you go. Every day, consciously look for things to be grateful for, and express your gratitude heartily. Keep your eyes and heart open to see the beauty in the world around you, and praise God for it. Your life will be enriched and filled with joy and satisfaction. The keys to God's storehouse of treasures are praise and thanksgiving.

It is impossible to live with a constant attitude of praise and thanksgiving and be depressed at the same time. As you thank God for His blessings of grace, He will release more and more to you.

Lord, today I want to express my praise to You for all the beauty that You have placed in my life.

~ Amen ~

OCTOBER 21

A beautiful heritage

LORD, you have assigned me my portion and my cup; you have made my lot secure. The boundary lines have fallen for me in pleasant places; surely I have a delightful inheritance. (Ps. 16:5-6)

David declares that all good things come from God. His praise reaches a joyful climax as he extols God for the glorious inheritance that he has received from the hand of God.

We have also received a glorious and delightful inheritance. We have so much to be grateful for: the beauty of blue skies; majestic mountains; surging oceans; the abundance and variety of plants and animals. As we consider the works of God's hands, our hearts overflow with songs of praise.

God has made known to us the path of life in every area of our lives: our families, our career and leisure time, our cultural heritage, the governing of our nation, the economy. We ask God to bless all the peoples of our land.

We pledge our hearts anew to love our country, our fellowmen, and our God. We serve our country with a love that seeks unity in the midst of diversity, morality without hypocrisy; with truth that is not self-serving. With such an attitude we will truly enjoy the inheritance that God has given us.

Creator God, I thank You for the beautiful inheritance that You have given to me. Help me to live in such a way that I glorify You as I live in my inheritance.

~ Amen ~

Expect great things from God

"Go home to your family and tell them how much the Lord has done for you, and how he has had mercy on you." (Mk. 5:19)

If you expect little from life, you will not achieve much spiritually or intellectually. Your deepest ambitions and desires will never be fulfilled unless you diligently and purposefully pursue them.

Perhaps you are too ready to say, "I can't" when you should be saying, "I'll give it a go." If you do not try you will spend your life wading through the shallow waters of mediocrity, oblivious that life has so much to offer.

If you have the courage to suck the marrow out of life, you will have great expectations. The enthusiasm that comes from a sense of anticipation, combined with a strong determination to achieve, will lead to success, satisfaction and happiness.

True greatness is measured by increasing cooperation with your heavenly Father. Once you have yielded yourself as an instrument in the hand of the Father, and you live each day to fulfill His will, you will find that spiritual depth, insight into life and a growing sensitivity will characterize your life.

In fellowship and unity with You, Father, I can achieve true greatness. Help me to learn to expect great things from You so that I can do great things for You.

~ Amen ~

OCTOBER 23

Gratitude glorifies God

I will praise you, O Lord, with all my heart; I will tell of all your wonders. (Ps. 9:1)

Be careful never to allow your faith to make you arrogant. Even though religion is a serious matter, some of God's most dedicated servants were lively, happy people. A faith that is void of humor can hardly express the spirit and attitude of Jesus Christ.

One of the most beautiful things we read about Jesus is that ordinary people enjoyed listening to Him and that children were at ease in His presence. This would not have been true had He been constantly gloomy. He emanated a deep peace and happiness, joy and quiet humor enabled Him to love and appreciate people.

Your sense of humor, enriched by your gratitude and love, is a gift from God. When you have the attitude of Jesus Christ, you learn to thank God with joy, and you will make the exciting discovery that there is true joy in serving Him and that gratitude and gladness can glorify God much more than verbosity and arrogance could ever do.

I am so grateful for the way in which Jesus revealed You to us, Father. Thank You for being approachable and for Your great love.

~ Amen ~

Spontaneous thanksgiving

Your ways, O God, are holy. What god is so great as our God? You are the God who performs miracles; you display your power among the peoples. (Ps. 77:13-14)

We serve a wonderful God and King! But, unfortunately, we sometimes lose sight of His greatness. Then we end up leading petty, unfulfilled lives. Instead of growing into the fullness of His stature through focusing on Him, we try to reduce Him to our level.

God is great and Scripture resounds with His invitation for us to share in His greatness. Jesus promised to dwell in those who love Him and to be revealed through them to the world. Surrendering to His presence transforms petty dwarves into spiritual giants. It requires steadfast faith in the promises of God and the courage to live out those promises to grow in Christ.

When you are aware of God living in you your attitude to life changes. Trust and confidence replace a sense of inferiority, love overcomes hate, compassion conquers bitterness. And as you honestly and sincerely acknowledge the greatness of God in you, your heart will overflow with gratitude for the glory and the beauty He imparts to your daily life.

Wondrous God, because You dwell in me through Jesus Christ I can overcome all the negative things in life and be filled with all the goodness of Your Holy Spirit.

~ Amen ~

OCTOBER 25

The power of thanksgiving

"Heal me, O Lord, and I shall be healed; Save me and I shall be saved, for you are the one I praise." (Jer. 17:14)

The person who has not raised his heart and voice to God in grateful praise, has missed out on one of the greatest experiences of life. It is sad that so many people consider praise and worship as a time of gloominess, something to be endured rather than enjoyed.

The psalmist appeals to all people, saying, *"Oh, clap your hands all you peoples! Shout to God with the voice of triumph!"* (Ps. 47:1). It is impossible to clap your hands and sing to the glory of God and still be gloomy. If you are feeling down-hearted, then start praising and thanking God now. It might seem foolish to you, but you can thank God that He is with you in your present situation.

True thanksgiving to the almighty God should not depend on your feelings. You don't need an organ or the church choir to truly praise and thank God. The simple lifting up of your heart to Him brings you straight into His presence and you cannot help but join with the angels surrounding His throne, singing His praise and glory.

I want to lift my heart to You and worship You with praise and thanksgiving for You alone are worthy.

~ Amen ~

The miraculous power of praise

OCTOBER 26

My heart is steadfast, O God; I will sing and make music with all my soul ... I will awaken the dawn. (Ps. 108:1-2)

We often lay our needs before God, and confess our sins and shortcomings to Him in prayer. Yet it is sad, but true, that we often neglect to express our praise and gratitude to Him in prayer.

Never underestimate the power of praise in your prayer life. If someone impresses you, you praise that person directly, or by telling others of what he has done. Good artists, sportsmen, musicians and singers are showered with praise.

Why shouldn't we then shower God with praise? Think of all the remarkable things that He has done; the miracles that flow from Him; the extraordinary scope of His love. Ponder for a moment the wonders of creation; of human life and achievement – and praise and glorify Him. He is, more than anyone else, worthy of our love and gratitude.

If you focus on praising and glorifying God, you will develop a very special relationship with the living Christ, which will transform your prayer life and intensify your love for Him. Through your praise you will become a stronger witness for Him.

Great and wonderful God, we want to exalt Your name forever, and praise and glorify You for all the wonders of Your love and grace that You give to us even though we don't deserve them.

~ Amen ~

When your burden gets heavy

I despise my life; I would not live forever. Let me alone; my days have no meaning. (Job 7:16)

When you are feeling dejected or sad, it is good to do something that will brighten someone's day. It might sound silly to you, but it is good therapy: it is impossible to make someone else happy without easing the pain in your own heart.

Take a good look at the world around you: there is always someone whose burden is heavier than yours. Perhaps there is someone in your circle of friends who requires help only you can give. It might just be possible that your own sorrow and grief have prepared you to help others more effectively.

Regardless of what has caused your despondency, God can use it to enrich the lives of others around you. Share your burdens with Him – He will never burden you with a cross that is too heavy for you to carry. He will lift the burden from your shoulders as you serve your fellowmen in love.

Don't fall into the pit of self-pity. That will deal a deathblow to loving others. If your love for God is true and sincere, you will love others and show it in your acts of service.

Savior, help me to see others with the eyes of Your compassion and to love them with Your grace and mercy.

~ Amen ~

Be thankful in everything

Better a little with the fear of the LORD than great wealth with turmoil. (Prov. 15:16)

Inspirational phrases such as, "Expect God to do great things," or "We serve a miracle-working God," or "Nothing is impossible to those who believe," stress the greatness of God. However, the average Christian is so busy looking for a spectacular revelation of the miracle-working God, that he is not able to see God at work in the common, everyday things. We find it difficult to believe that the good and beautiful things that happen to us come from our gracious God.

When you have learned to appreciate the small blessings from God you will see how God is at work in your life. The wonder of friendship, the kindness of people, an understanding heart that accepts you when others misunderstand you, the wonder of joy and laughter – are all expressions of the greatness and the blessings of God.

Make a decision never again to take anything for granted. Thank God for blessings as you become aware of them. By doing this, you will unlock the treasure room of God, and fill your life with new beauty and riches.

I praise and thank You, gracious Lord, for the small things that make each day so delightful. Help me never again to take daily blessings for granted.

~ Amen ~

OCTOBER 29

Show your gratitude

"I am Jesus, whom you are persecuting," he replied.
(Acts 9:5)

Many people who read of Jesus Christ's life in the gospels, are amazed at the way people treated Him. He emanated goodness, compassion, sympathy and love and yet, through His whole ministry, He was opposed and criticized. The religious leaders hated Him and were continually looking for ways to destroy Him. When He was eventually crucified, people mocked Him and His most intimate friends denied Him.

People today are dismayed at the way the Prince of Peace was treated. After all, He only wanted the very best for each one of us.

Christ is still being persecuted. When you participate in activities that grieve Jesus the Lord, when you ignore the needs of your fellowmen – then you are persecuting Jesus Christ in the same way others did centuries ago.

Through sacrificing His life, Christ gave you the gift of salvation. All He asks from you in return is to gratefully surrender your life to Him so that you can find the absolute joy of life in Christ.

Savior and Friend, I want to show You how grateful I am for all You have done for me by sharing Your love and joy with others. I surrender my life to You.

~ Amen ~

Grateful obedience

Shout for joy to the LORD, all the earth. (Ps. 100:1)

Many people feel that Christianity is a life of hardship and that they have to sacrifice so many things to follow Christ. They forget that when they lay down their old life and start a new life in Christ Jesus, that it is a life of indescribable joy and gladness. When God asks us to lay down our old life, we can be confident that He will replace it with something much better.

When God requires total obedience, life will not lose its joy and gladness. He promised to bear our burdens if we obey and trust Him. Trust Him completely so that depression and anxiety will vanish under the influence of a positive and cheerful faith.

Many of God's servants have great responsibilities, but they don't bear them on their own, because they know that His everlasting arms are constantly supporting them.

If God has given you a special responsibility, don't become despondent and think that life has become a burden. Rejoice in the Lord and in His power and accept your duty with gratitude.

I want to accept my task with gladness, Lord, because You have done so much for me.

~ Amen ~

OCTOBER 31

Serve the Lord with gladness!

Worship the LORD with gladness; come before him with joyful songs. (Ps. 100:2)

I praise and thank You, Father, because You created me and then You made me a new creation in Christ. How awesome it is to call You my Father. Thank You for the beauty of creation through which You speak to me and where I can draw close to You in worship.

I bow before You in gratitude for Your Son, Jesus and for sending Him into this sin-torn world to save sinners and make them children of God. Thank You, Lord Jesus, that You suffered and died and rose triumphant from the dead. I praise You for the gift of the Holy Spirit who led me to Jesus and who continues to guide me.

With gratitude I praise You for Your Word, through which the Holy Spirit reveals Your divine will for my life.

I praise and thank You, my Father, for abundant blessings: for my family, my friends and all the things that make my life worthwhile. Give me a grateful heart always, O Lord, so that my life may be a song of thanksgiving to Your glory.

I want to sing to the glory of the Lord as long as I live. You have done great things and You are worthy of all praise.

~ Amen ~

November

Almighty God and loving Father,
every day we are surrounded by uncertainty
about many things: our health, our family,
our work, our finances, our future,
and even our relationship with You.
Thank You that Your Holy Spirit teaches
us to say: "I know for certain that Jesus lives!"
He redeemed me and made me His child;
in His hands, I am safe, for time and eternity.
Lord, You alone know how doubt still sometimes
festers; how my trust in You is often tested
and how dearly I want to believe
like the faith heroes of old.
I thank You for all the means of grace
that You give to strengthen my faith:
the sacraments of Baptism and Communion;
the Bible and prayer, worshiping in church
and fellowship in faith; faithful friends who
intercede with You that my faith will not falter.

~ Amen ~

A God who encourages

May the God who gives endurance and encouragement give you a spirit of unity among yourselves as you follow Christ Jesus. (Rom. 15:5)

We all feel heavy and depressed at one time or another. For no apparent reason you cannot handle the demands of life any more and you give in to despair. Everything you try seems to fail, you become discouraged and feel inadequate to cope with life's struggles.

When you've come to the end of your own abilities, it is good to spend time quietly in the presence of God and there receive the encouragement that only He can give. Be still and surrender yourself anew to Him. Remember that He is God, and you will be strengthened by His encouragement.

In the silence of His divine presence, you can recall all His glorious promises of encouragement. Remember that in both the storm and the stillness, God, in Christ Jesus, is with you. He will give you the strength to complete the task He has given you to do.

God does not want you to remain in the dark valley of despondency. He will give you the encouragement that will make your life meaningful and beautiful once again.

Holy God, when life is too much for me, I withdraw into Your presence and there find the comfort and the strength I need.

~ Amen ~

The scourge of discouragement

Though he stumble, he will not fall, for the LORD upholds him with his hand. (Ps. 37:24)

People become discouraged when disappointment or failure destroys a cherished dream, or when noble ideals and plans collapse like a house of cards. If discouragement settles in your heart you may become bitter and find it difficult to hold onto your vision.

If you are discouraged because a plan has failed, carefully assess the idea. If you are convinced that the idea is bigger than your discouragement, you can reject the discouragement as the nonsense it really is. Always keep the vision of what you are trying to attain clearly in your mind, and do not allow it to be suppressed by thoughts of failure.

It is important to retain an inner strength that helps you to control your negative thoughts. When your mind is sound and healthy, you will be able to deal appropriately with negative thoughts.

Applying Christ's teachings and being guided by His indwelling Spirit form the foundation on which you can base your decision to fight discouragement, so that you can achieve the goal that burns brightly in your heart.

I praise You, Lord my God and Father, that I am able to combat discouragement successfully with Your help.

~ Amen ~

The blessing of dependence

"And I'll say to myself, 'You have plenty of good things laid up for many years. Take life easy; eat, drink and be merry.'" (Lk. 12:19)

We are all deeply dependent upon God but many people ignore this truth. The Holy Spirit enters our lives when we accept this truth; when we realize that our happiness does not depend upon our own efforts and achievements, but upon God and God alone.

Could there be any "happiness" when you surrender control of your own life? Christ says, "Yes!" It brings an extraordinary happiness that blesses your life abundantly. A kind of happiness that enables you to gain the kingdom of God. It is a deep, quiet happiness that brings peace to your life.

It is to be secure in God. To be assured that Somebody loves you and cares about you. That He holds you with a strong hand, a hand with nail-scars that bear witness to His great love for you. When you can voice the same sentiments as Christ, "Yet not as I will, but as you will" you will experience the true depths of happiness that are the result of unconditional surrender to Christ and His will for your life.

Help me, Lord Jesus, to store up treasures for myself in heaven where moth and rust do not destroy.

~ Amen ~

Discouraged?

Say to those with fearful hearts, "Be strong, do not fear; your God will come." (Is. 35:4)

We all feel discouraged at times. It manifests itself in different ways, but always leaves you disillusioned, wondering whether all your efforts were worth the trouble. Only those who strive for a goal can be discouraged. If you feel that your dreams have been destroyed and your efforts have come to nothing, do not allow self-pity to sow the seed of discouragement in your spirit. There are spiritual reserves from which you can draw, and which will give you hope and a sense of purpose.

God is your constant source of inspiration and encouragement. He asks only that you come and draw freely from Him. Then you will be able to overcome discouragement. Remember: God is waiting to work in harmony with you. He does not work against you, but seeks your cooperation at all times so that you can overcome the effects of discouragement and move forward toward your goal.

You do not fight alone against discouragement and depression. God is on your side and He is ready to lift you up so that you can continue with joy and triumph gloriously.

I thank You, heavenly Father, that through the power of Your Spirit, I can triumph over discouragement.

~ Amen ~

God's silences

Yet when he [Jesus] heard that Lazarus was sick, he stayed where he was two more days. (Jn. 11:6)

There are many devout Christians who, like Peter, constantly want to remain on the mountaintop with Jesus. When they occasionally become despondent, they feel that they have somehow disappointed God. But Christians are ordinary people who are subject to the fluctuations of the heart. You may have wonderful mountaintop experiences followed suddenly by a lunge into the valleys of despair. We tend to think that the presence of God is found only on the mountaintops, but this is not so.

Whatever your changing moods, God remains unchangeable. When you are in the depths of despair ask yourself, "What is God trying to show me in this situation?"

Many of God's most devout followers discovered His will for their lives when they were struggling in the dark valleys. Do not think you have failed spiritually just because you are feeling despondent. Rather try to understand God's will for your life. Don't become afraid if God is silent and appears to be distant. He is just as close to you as when you were with Him on the mountaintop.

Ever-present God, help me to experience the reality of Your presence, even when I feel far away from You.

~ Amen ~

NOVEMBER 6

A reason to live

"Because I live, you also will live." (Jn. 14:19)

In these ominous times in which we live many people wonder whether life is worthwhile. They are terrified about an unknown future, and dejection rules their minds. But life is extremely precious and even the most despondent person realizes this when his or her life is threatened.

Despite how gloomy the future seems, it is important to remember that your life and future are in the hands of God. The Christian's life is not ruled by blind fate. God is in control of every situation in which you find yourself. He knows your needs and is always able to provide for you. As your faith grows and you begin to trust Him more and more, you will also begin to experience the joy of a life in Christ and be comforted by the presence of the unfailing and unchanging God.

Through His death and resurrection Jesus not only gave you life, but also a reason to live. Through His Holy Spirit He provides you with the skills to cope with life. Choose life and live it in the abundance of Jesus Christ, giving Him the glory.

Faithful Lord, in the midst of the change and the corruption that I see around me daily, I know that Jesus lives and that He has made it worthwhile for me to be alive.

~ Amen ~

Light in the darkness

NOVEMBER 7

To those who have been called, who are loved by God the Father and kept by Jesus Christ: Mercy, peace and love be yours in abundance. (Jude 1-2)

The world seems to have been in a state of chaos since the beginning of time. And lawlessness and violence seem to increase steadily. The cost of living continues to climb and people live in fear and insecurity. What is the solution to this sad state of affairs?

There is only one solution: confidently place your faith and trust in Jesus Christ. He has conquered a dark and hostile world and replaced fear with love. He has restored hope where circumstances appeared to be hopeless. To those who believe in Him He has given the blessing of His peace that transcends all understanding.

This is your answer to the distressing confusion and fear of our time. Believe in Jesus Christ and His promises; place your trust in Him unconditionally and He will lead you from the darkness into the light of His unfathomable love. If you do this you will no longer worry about the future because you will be protected by the peace of God.

Thank You, Lord my God, that You grant perfect peace to Your children in this dark world. Thank You that I can experience this inner peace because I trust in You.

~ Amen ~

Your divine companion

The righteous cry out, and the LORD hears them; he delivers them from all their troubles. (Ps. 34:17)

Many people struggle with loneliness caused by varying circumstances: the loss of a loved one; a serious illness; struggling with problems when friends seem to have forsaken you. These are only some of the reasons that people sometimes feel lonely and despondent.

When you find yourself in such circumstances, Satan tries to sow seeds of doubt, discouragement and despair in your heart. Then you begin to feel that there is no hope, and soon you slump into the depths of self-pity and despair.

But the experience of godly people throughout the centuries shows that we are never alone. The hand of God rests on you always. Hold on to His assurance that He is always with you.

When it seems as if life is treating you unfairly, don't give up hope. Rather lay your fears and worries at the feet of the living Christ. Open your heart and life to the Holy Spirit and He will fan the flame of hope once again. Then the tiny flame that threatened to die out will burn brightly to light your path.

Powerful Redeemer, grant me the strength to keep my hand firmly in Yours even under the most difficult circumstances. Lead me from the darkness into Your wonderful light.

~ Amen ~

Be strong

Wait for the Lord; be strong and take heart and wait for the Lord. (Ps. 27:14)

Sometimes sickness, affliction, worries, death, disappointment, old age and hardships make the path through life steep and the future seem uncertain.

In the dark hours of his life, David found that the Lord was the strength of his life. Even though clouds sometimes blot out the sun, you need not dwell in darkness. Where the Lord is, there is always light. *"You, O Lord, keep my lamp burning; my God turns my darkness into light."* (Ps. 18:28).

Even though you may feel hopelessly ensnared in your crises, the Lord will save you from all your distress and anxiety, even though you don't know when and how. *"From six calamities he will rescue you; in seven no harm will befall you."* (Job 5:19).

The Lord is your refuge, a place to which you can flee in times of danger and where you will find safety and rest. *"I will say of the Lord, 'He is my refuge and my fortress, my God, in whom I trust.'"* (Ps. 91:2). May the love of the Lord encourage you always.

Omnipotent Father, because You are my strength, my Savior and my refuge, I will not give in to despair. Thank You that I can find refuge in You.

~ Amen ~

God has a plan for you

NOVEMBER 10

And now, do not be distressed and do not be angry with yourselves for selling me here, because it was to save lives that God sent me ahead of you. (Gen. 45:5)

It is often difficult to understand that God is fulfilling His plan in your life, especially when times are tough. When Joseph was sold into slavery, and when an unscrupulous woman robbed him of his freedom he probably struggled to discern God's will. Nevertheless, many years later, he recognized that God had been with him through it all.

If you are in the deep waters of affliction right now, remember that it might be part of God's tapestry. He determines the pattern of your life. In your darkest hour, keep believing that, in spite of the way things seem, God is still in control because you have committed your life to Him.

God can give purpose and meaning to Joseph's slavery, Moses' depression, Jeremiah's lamentations – and yes, even to Jesus' death on the cross. Life's darkest moments can become a testimony of God's perfect purpose for your life.

In your present circumstances, difficult as they might be, hold on to the assurance that God is busy working out His perfect plan for your life.

Faithful Guide, I will trust You to lead me surely along the pathways through life, even when dark shadows hide my way.

~ *Amen* ~

Light up your life

When Jesus spoke again to the people, he said, "I am the light of the world. Whoever follows me will never walk in darkness, but will have the light of life." (Jn. 8:12)

Darkness affects people in many different ways. Prolonged and utter darkness can cause fear, depression, loneliness and sorrow. When light comes, whether natural or artificial, it brings relief and a feeling of safety.

The darkness of the soul has a similar negative effect on people. People lose hope. Sickness, death, disappointment and sorrow can plunge our emotions to the darkest depths of despair. The light of hope and peace flickers and dims when we face afflictions and trials. And this often leads to despondency, depression and despair.

The only way in which you will manage to fight against, and overcome, these dark shadows, is through steadfast faith in God. Turn to Christ in every situation in life. Trust Him and believe that He will guide you through the particular problem you are experiencing right now. Rather than cursing the darkness, light a small candle of faith and help to light up the darkness.

Walk in His light and soon you will find that the darkness has fled. With His light in your heart, each day becomes radiant for you.

Loving Guide, while You hold my hand I am safe and secure. Strengthen my faith daily.

~ Amen ~

Conquer depression through faith

NOVEMBER 12

"But for you who revere my name, the sun of righteousness will rise with healing in its wings." (Mal. 4:2)

Depression and pessimism are ailments that can destroy the soul. Apart from the fact that depression is an illness of the mind, it also affects your physical and spiritual well-being, limits your vision of the future, and negatively influences your attitude to life. The causes of depression are numerous and include fear, anxiety, illness, financial instability and loneliness.

You may attempt to fight the condition with manmade remedies, but their effect will only be temporary. Sooner or later the effects will wear off and your condition will return, often with a vengeance.

The only way to fight such an emotional disruption effectively is to turn to Christ and to open yourself to His love and healing influence. Accept Him as Lord of your life and put yourself in His care unconditionally. This will require immense faith, but when Jesus takes control of your life and guides you along the path you need to take through life, you will find that, because of your obedience to Him, you will be filled with a sense of self-confidence and well-being that only He can give you.

I cling to You, Lord Jesus, in the knowledge that nothing in this life can harm me as long as You are with me.

~ Amen ~

Light from the darkness

When all the people saw this, they fell prostrate and cried, "The LORD – he is God! The LORD – he is God!" (1 Kgs. 18:39)

Today, as in the days of Elijah, it takes an earth-shattering experience for some people to recognize the existence and omnipotence of God. People become used to a way of life that has little or no space for the Lord.

And yet God moves in mysterious ways to reveal the wonders of His love. Sometimes He uses drastic measures and we should not judge the Lord with our limited understanding, but trust Him for His mercy.

Perhaps you have experienced adversity or tragedy or maybe your burden seems unbearable and your problems unsolvable. Don't give in to the temptation to throw in the towel, but turn in faith to the living Christ. He was a human being just like you. He knows all about your situation, understands your distress, and is ready to come to your assistance.

Christ experienced the torment of crucifixion so that people could be drawn to Him. The One who leads you out of distress still sometimes uses adverse circumstances to draw you closer to His heart. Accept this and live in peace in the certainty of His love.

You, wonderful God and loving Father, have a perfect plan with every life, including mine.

God is with you

NOVEMBER 14

"The LORD your God is with you, he is mighty to save. He will take great delight in you, he will quiet you with his love, he will rejoice over you with singing." (Zeph. 3:17)

When things go wrong in your life it is easy to give up and despair. The battle that you are fighting seems so unfair. Many people once seemed invincible, but were later overwhelmed by a spirit of helplessness and hopelessness.

If ever there was a time when everything seemed hopeless, it was on the day of Jesus' crucifixion. The hopes and dreams of those who thought that He would be the Savior of Israel were dashed when He died like a common criminal on the cross.

But then God intervened. The Lord God, who was Christ's hope and strength, miraculously turned apparent defeat into victory. The distress of Good Friday was transformed into the triumphant resurrection of Easter Sunday when Christ rose majestically from the dead.

Whatever circumstances you find yourself in; however dismal the future may seem and despite all the problems that confront you, remember that God is with you and in control of your circumstances. Trust in Him and He will grant you victory.

Redeemer and Friend, thank You that I can be sure, through You, that God loves me and is always with me.

~ Amen ~

Jesus illuminates the darkness

Let him who walks in the dark, who has no light, trust in the name of the LORD and rely on his God. (Is. 50:10)

There comes a time in everyone's life when the path ahead seems dark; when difficulties overwhelm you and you become despondent because despair and darkness seem to surround you. Often your circumstances are so desperate that you feel completely helpless and simply cannot free yourself from the darkness. In these circumstances you are at your most vulnerable and pressurized.

Despite how far from God you feel in times like these, you must remember the glorious truth that He is actually closer to you than ever before. Your heavenly Father has assured you that He will never abandon or forsake you. He is constantly by your side, waiting for you to turn to Him for help, which He is always ready and willing to provide.

Regardless of what is happening in your life, even when you are unable to pray, you can still turn to Christ and lay your fears and concerns before Him. Because He lived on earth as a man, He is all too aware of the difficulties and problems that you experience. Allow Him to lead you and you will experience the blessing and joy of His love and peace.

O Lord, please send Your light and Your truth to me; let it guide me to Your holy mountain so that I can enter Your holy presence.

~ Amen ~

Trust in God

NOVEMBER 16

"My grace is sufficient for you, for my power is made perfect in weakness." (2 Cor. 12:9)

There are very few people who have not, at times, been aware of the inadequacy of their own resourcefulness, and who thus feel that they simply cannot continue. These feelings may be the result of illness, death, loneliness, financial insecurity or any of the numerous setbacks that can have a destructive influence on the human mind and emotions.

In so many cases people regard their situation as hopeless, and they run the risk of feeling completely defeated. Whatever the predicament in which you find yourself, and however dark the outlook, never underestimate the extent of God's love for you and the expanse of His grace.

Take a moment to consider some of the numerous instances in the Bible and in history when God transformed despair into hope, and defeat into victory through His grace. However desperate your circumstances may seem to you, always remember that God loves you with an eternal love, and that He is waiting for you to turn to Him and trust in Him. Your faith will be rewarded, and, in His own wonderful way, He will deliver you.

Faithful God and Father, through the years You have proved Yourself to be faithful. Therefore I will hold on to Your hand in the future, because Your grace is sufficient for me at all times and under all circumstances.

~ Amen ~

Love fills the heart with hope

Brothers, we do not want you to ... grieve like the rest of men who have no hope. (1 Thes. 4:13)

Love ... always hopes. (1 Cor. 13:6-7)

Hope and despair are found in the hearts of people and not in circumstances. Love is so important because it causes hope to triumph. When things are at their darkest, hope rises through love to light the darkness of night. There is no room for despair; God has enough love to avert it. Hope is woven into the nature of man so that we can trust in the future.

Martin Luther said that everything done in the world is done in hope. Farmers sow in the hope of reaping a harvest. People marry because they hope for a happy family life. Business people work hard because they hope for the fruit of their labors.

What oxygen does for the body, hope does for the soul: without it we would die. When all is hopeless, then hope keeps us going. Hope strengthens the soul so we can hold onto eternity and onto the love of God. Praise the Lord, for He is good. His love is infinite. He gives us hope out of love.

Let me never believe that anyone is hopelessly lost, because, in love, You sent Your Son to save the lost, O Lord.

~ Amen ~

Dealing with adversity

NOVEMBER 18

"Come close to me." When they had done so, he said, "I am you brother Joseph, the one you sold into Egypt! God sent me ahead of you ... to save your lives by a great deliverance." (Gen. 45:4, 7)

At times Joseph must have felt that God had forsaken him. His brothers tried to destroy him and his dreams, he was kidnapped and taken to a foreign land. But, after many years, he could state with conviction that God had been at work for his good through all these adversities.

Being a child of God does not safeguard you against adversity and heartache. You are subject to the same trials and tribulations as everyone – the good and the wicked. When you are gloriously aware that God is your Father, you will realize that He uses difficulties to your advantage. Knowing this gives you the spiritual strength to persevere.

As you grow in the knowledge of God, you will see how He works in the ordinary things in life. Instead of complaining when problems come your way, you will steadfastly believe that God reveals His omnipotence, even in the most trying circumstances. Patiently allow Him to weave His holy will in your life and, despite all your disappointments and problems, He will achieve His perfect purpose.

You are my only shelter, Lord, and I am helpless before You. You deliver me from evil and guide me when I am surrounded by darkness and am devoid of all hope.

~ Amen ~

"I know for certain!"

"He will never leave you nor forsake you." (Deut. 31:6)

When Joshua was appointed as Moses' successor he received the blessed assurance that God would never leave him nor forsake him. Joshua led the people of Israel into the Promised Land with the promise that God would be by his side in all circumstances.

You probably have a number of friends who are trustworthy and who support you in times of need, and yet there are times when even they do not live up to your expectations.

The Lord is so reassuringly different. If you need comfort, the Lord is ready to give it to you. If you need guidance in a confusing situation, the Lord will show you what to do. If you need inspiration for a difficult task or decision, the Lord will guide you.

Are you tired, troubled or confused? Does the road ahead seem strewn with problems, concerns and troubles? Ask the Lord to help you and you will discover the truth of Deuteronomy 31:6. He will grant you peace and joy in abundance. If you ask Him, you will find that the Lord is as faithful as He promised in His Word.

God our Father, thank You that I have the assurance that You will never fail me nor forsake me. Forgive me for the times when I failed and disappointed You.
~ Amen ~

NOVEMBER 20

Christ is always available

"And surely I am with you always, to the very end of the age." (Mt. 28:20)

One of the glorious truths of the gospel is that Christ is always there for His followers. This is a comforting assurance when we are overcome by an inexplicable melancholy.

The comforting truth is that the Lord is with you wherever you are. He is with you as you strive to get to know Him better and to break through the barriers of doubt and uncertainty. He invites us to lay aside our self-made fears and doubts and rest in Him, the One who alone gives peace to restless souls.

All Christians who accept this gracious invitation will need to let go of their pet sins. Unfortunately, there are those who want to enter the presence of the living Christ on their own terms. This cannot work because we can only experience and enjoy His presence if we meet His requirements.

Christianity is based on accepting Christ as your living Savior. Without that, your faith has no foundation and you will be unable to live abundantly. Through the working of the Holy Spirit you become aware of the presence of Christ with every step that you take through life.

Thank You, loving Father, that You are always available and that I can experience Your presence every day of my life.

~ Amen ~

Walk in the light

This is the message we have heard from him and declare to you: God is light; in him there is no darkness at all. (1 Jn. 1:5)

Many things that happen in the world today are symptoms of a sick society. Those who are sober-minded and sensitive are shocked by the atrocities and scandals that confront us daily. The average person feels inadequate to confront the evil around them. This can give rise to an attitude of despair and people start believing that nothing can be done about it.

If you have a vibrant faith in God and are willing to put your trust in Him unconditionally, believing that He can overcome all evil, you will soon find the darkness in your heart beginning to lift. When Jesus Christ lived on earth, God's love broke through the darkest moment in history on that first Good Friday when He overcame the forces of evil. He rose triumphantly from the dead on Easter morning.

Nothing in our modern world can be as appalling as the crucifixion on Golgotha. And yet the Light broke through. Regardless of how dark your circumstances may be, put your trust in Christ, follow Him and you will see how His light expels the darkness from your life.

Lord Jesus, in Your light we can see light. Help us to see Your light in this dark world so that the darkness will be dispersed.

~ Amen ~

The greatest inspiration

NOVEMBER 22

"But you will receive power when the Holy Spirit comes on you." (Acts 1:8)

Inspiration is a wonderful asset and blessing. When you are inspired you can accomplish more than normal. Perhaps the source of your inspiration is listening to a stirring sermon or inspiring music. This gives you a burst of new-found energy. Someone whose emotions constantly fluctuate needs constant inspiration. Often a vicious circle of inspiration and depression forms, and the person is seldom on an even keel. True godly inspiration is lasting and has the ability to overcome depression. It gives you the ability to function even when doubts lurk in your heart and mind.

Through the indwelling of the Holy Spirit, Christ becomes the constant source of inspiration to all who accept Him as Savior and Redeemer. This inspiration is not subject to our changing moods but is constant and eternal.

Unless the outcome of the inspiration you receive is passed on to others around you, it won't last very long. Allow the Spirit of Christ to flow through you to inspire and to bless all those with whom you come into contact.

Lord, please let the inspiration of the Holy Spirit flow through my life so that Your peace can flow from my heart and bless others.

~ Amen ~

Together with God

I can do everything through him who gives me strength. (Phil. 4:13)

When you think of God in all His glory and of yourself as an insignificant speck on the earth, it is incredibly difficult to identify with Him. And yet the Spirit of God, who fills God's entire creation, can also inhabit your spirit. When you realize this, you release a previously untapped power in your life.

When you realize that God has revealed Himself in you through His Spirit, you will learn to draw on His strength, and your life will be vibrant and balanced. You will also realize that your life should live up to His expectations. You no longer live to please yourself, but to do His will. Through the grace of God you can attain this kind of life in the strength of the Lord Jesus Christ.

Before our Savior ascended to heaven He promised that He would send His Spirit to those who accept Him as Savior and Lord and who yield to His Spirit. It is the Holy Spirit who makes God a reality in the life of the Christian and who enables him to live in harmony with God.

Merciful Lord Jesus, I accept the gift of the Holy Spirit and therefore enjoy intimate communion with You, my Lord and my God.

~ Amen ~

For days when everything goes wrong

"To whom do you belong, and where are you going, and who owns all these animals in front of you?" (Gen. 32:17)

Life must have purpose and significance if you are to live meaningfully. Maybe you have been doing the same work for years, and as far as you can see you will be doing it for many years to come. What, you may justifiably ask, is the use of thinking that circumstances will change? You feel trapped in a dead-end street from which you will never be able to escape.

One of the great truths of the Christian life is that it changes your attitude. Previously you lived without hope or expectation, but Christ now plants new hope in your heart. When you truly start living in Christ, you look at life with new understanding.

You will never again have to ask, "Is life worthwhile?" When the thoughts of Christ fill you and the Holy Spirit's strength saturates your spirit, you realize the rich quality of your faith, and your life takes on new and exciting dimensions.

Lord Jesus, You came so that we may have life in abundance. Help me to remember to come to You when days are dark, so that my life may be infused with significance and meaning once again.

~ Amen ~

Sufficient grace for you

You then, my son, be strong in the grace that is in Christ Jesus. (2 Tim. 2:1)

Many people are not able to work through setbacks in life. When a serious problem occurs, they collapse. They try to flee from the reality of personal crises. Anxiety and concern rob them of peace because they try to solve problems in their own strength.

Christ invites all those who are weary and burdened to bring their problems to Him and they will find rest for their souls. He invites you to cast your cares on Him because He cares for you. Turn to God and He will equip you to handle your problems with confidence.

Regardless of what your circumstances in life may be, regardless of how anxious you are about seemingly insoluble problems, don't run away from them in panic and despair, but confront them with Christ at your side. Receive your strength and confidence from Him. Regardless of how alarming the problem may seem, you can know for certain that God's strength will be revealed in your weakness. Under all circumstances His grace will be sufficient for you and you will be able to deal with your problems with confidence.

Father, I ask You for strength to carry the load that is upon me today. Strengthen me so that I can move forward with confidence.

~ Amen ~

God's grace and your problems

In all your ways acknowledge him, and he will make your paths straight. (Prov. 3:6)

Life can suddenly become filled with problems. Regardless of where they come from, they will dominate your life until you find a solution.

Discussing a problem with a trusted friend often puts it in the right perspective, causing it to lose its overwhelming character. There are, however, some people who love to talk about their problems, while secretly hoping never to find a solution, because then there won't be much left to talk about.

If you are experiencing a problem and sincerely seek a solution, turn to God and don't focus on the problem. You cannot find a solution to your problem if you do not want to allow God to assist you.

Tell God about your problem, and testify to the greatness of God. Allow Him to create order out of chaos and to give you the right solution. You will be inspired with spiritual power because God is occupying His rightful place in your life and you and your circumstances are subjected to His grace. You will find solutions to your problems and by His grace you will live victoriously.

Eternal God, I put You first in my life, knowing that You alone are great and able to show me the way forward.

~ Amen ~

Find strength and comfort in the Word

Open my eyes that I may see wonderful things in your law. (Ps. 119:18)

Disillusionment and dejection are common. Many people are unhappy and depressed. They have developed a melancholy outlook on life.

In order to live and not merely exist, it is essential to nurture a positive attitude. When everything goes well, enjoy life and be cheerful. Praise God. But when things do not go well, analyze the circumstances and identify where things went wrong and then try to do something about it.

Your faith will need to be strong if you are to triumph over problems with joy. Such a faith comes through diligent prayer, when you seek the help of the living Christ.

Search the Scriptures for evidence of the wonderful work of almighty God. You will find example upon example of the ways in which ordinary people, like you and me, overcame hostile forces in the Name of the Lord. Draw comfort from the Word and, through the incarnate Word, Jesus Christ, you will be able to triumph over any adversity.

You reveal Yourself in Your Word. It is trustworthy, steadfast and unfailing. Thank You that I can know the life that is found in Your Word.

~ Amen ~

NOVEMBER 28

Live one day at a time

*"For today the L*ORD *will appear to you."* (Lev. 9:4)

You may, at times, think about deepening your prayer life and being more diligent in your Bible study. But other things come up and claim your attention. Your noble aspirations are eventually pushed so far into the background that they are almost forgotten. Despite your best efforts you slip back into the old rut, once again tasting the bitterness of failure and disappointment.

If you are determined to reestablish your spiritual goals, don't start by making impressive resolutions you know will be difficult to keep. Learn the secret of living one day at a time and offering your very best to God throughout that day. You will still have a sense of dissatisfaction because your best seems so inferior to God's holiness and perfection. The secret of living one day at a time for God is to do so in the strength of the living Christ. Spend time with Christ in the early hours of each day and use this time well. It will place the entire day in the right perspective, and you will discover that as you experience every day in His presence, you will grow spiritually and your life will become more meaningful.

Holy God, I want to live each day in Your holy presence so that I may grow spiritually and become stronger every day.

~ Amen ~

Your strength in difficult times

Let the word of Christ dwell in you richly. (Col. 3:16)

How do you survive when everyhing goes horribly wrong? How do you cope with financial setbacks, family crises, illness or death? Do you remain calm and collected, or do you flounder in a sea of doubt, confusion and despair?

Any of these things can cause you serious anxiety and concern. Your perspective can easily become skewed, and your disorganized thoughts may be unable to handle the situation logically or sensibly. There is a fundamental danger that you will make the wrong decisions or follow an inappropriate course of action, which will ultimately turn out to be damaging and will leave you riddled with guilt.

In order to live in peace and to be prepared for any eventuality, it is essential for you to maintain an intimate relationship with your Savior. To know of Him is one thing, but for the sake of your peace of mind you should know Him personally. Develop an awareness of His presence at all times and in all places. In this way you will ensure that His Spirit will continually work in you and sustain you in your difficult times.

Lord Jesus, You call everyone who is tired and overburdened to come to You. I accept Your invitation with gratitude and praise.

~ Amen ~

The power of inspired thoughts

Above all else, guard your heart, for it is the wellspring of life. (Prov. 4:23)

Our thoughts control our lives. A person who thinks positively acts constructively. Without purpose, our thoughts wander aimlessly, often with disastrous consequences. Having an active mind does not guarantee success. Many intelligent people miss the true purpose of life because they do not understand that their spirit governs their thoughts.

If your spirit harbors thoughts of bitterness, hate, and envy, your mind will be drenched with negative and destructive thoughts, and you will never experience the dynamism of the Christian faith. By living in harmony with the living Christ and allowing His Spirit to become an inspiration to your spirit, you can achieve the impossible.

The Lord graciously challenges us to, *"Remain in me, and I will remain in you"* (Jn. 15:4). To remain in Christ means to embrace Christ's ways with joy. It requires a healthy and profound prayer life, supported by faithful Bible study. This gives your mind the inspiration and strength that are only experienced by those who have put Jesus Christ first in their lives.

Through Your enabling grace, Lord Jesus, my mind is opened to the inspiration of the Holy Spirit.

~ Amen ~

December

Emmanuel! We worship You, Jesus Christ,
as "God with us!" Let us rejoice
and celebrate Christmas
with a holy attitude. Purify our spirits
of all hatred and bitterness; cleanse us of all sin
through the blood of the Lamb.
Let every gift we give be accompanied by
sincere love, as You gave Yourself as a gift to us.
Let every Christmas carol be sung with new
meaning, and let Your eternal Gospel
once again touch our hearts with benevolence.
Let the peace of which the angels sang
not remain merely an idle dream,
but let it become a glorious reality
through our faith. Let the miracle of Christmas
live on in our hearts when we return to our
everyday life. We pray this
in the Name of Him of whom the angels sang,
*"Glory to God in the highest, and on earth peace
to men on whom his favor rests"* (Lk. 2:14).

~ Amen ~

Experience the joy of the Lord!

Then the children of Israel – the priests and the Levites and the rest of the exiles – celebrated the dedication of the house of God with joy. (Ezra 6:16)

There are two attitudes toward Christianity that can cause immeasurable damage to your faith in God. The first is to see worship as an unpleasant duty, and the second is to become so blasé that you lose sight of the awesomeness of God.

Serving God and worshiping Him are not simply duties to perform, but an awesome privilege. To enter into the presence of God, the King of kings, you simply need to bow before Him in prayer. Through the living Christ, He is willing to come into your life.

Regular attendance of services or places of worship must never be allowed to turn you into a passive spectator. During times of worship remember that you are in the presence of the most holy God. Like Moses, you are at the burning bush of God's divine presence.

Enjoy your life with Christ. Allow Him to become part of your daily life. Then you will discover the fullness of life which He offers you in John 10:10, "*The thief comes only to steal and kill and destroy; I have come that they may have life, and have it to the full."*

Lord, I want my worship to be filled with an awareness of Your holiness. Help me never to lose sight of who You truly are.

~ Amen ~

DECEMBER 2

The joy of faith

But he who unites himself with the Lord is one with him in spirit. (1 Cor. 6:17)

Joy and gladness are not the main goals of the Christian faith, but an important by-product of it. The focus and purpose of our faith is the Lord Himself. When His life-giving Spirit fills your heart, the joy of a Christ-filled life becomes yours.

For this to be a reality in your life you need to develop a relationship with Christ. A personal and intimate relationship with Christ will fill your life with His peace and power. This begins when you accept His forgiveness for your sins and begin to live a life that reflects His nature.

Forgiveness and a Spirit-filled life bring great joy to all who strive to live "in Christ". And the culmination of this joy is to live in the constant awareness of the presence of God. You find yourself in fellowship with Him at all times, in all places. The more you become aware of His closeness, the stronger and more meaningful your faith gets. Then joy unspeakable and full of glory will flow from you in service to your fellowman.

I want to express my gratitude to You for Your closeness by living a life that glorifies You in every way.

~ Amen ~

Be a joyful Christian

Do everything without complaining or arguing. (Phil. 2:14)

The Christian life is one of service and submission. You may be called to work among needy people, or your calling might involve administration, preaching or another form of service. Whatever it is, it will require a sacrifice of your time and yourself.

Unfortunately so many people serve Christ with heavy and begrudging hearts. They do their work and often do it well, but they are unpleasant people with poor interpersonal skills. This spoils the quality of their deeds, which should manifest the compassion and mercy of Christ. People hesitate to approach them for help because of their negative attitude.

Whatever task you are assigned to do for Jesus is to be done to His glory. To ensure that you reflect the glory and love of God in everything that you do, do everything in the strength of the Holy Spirit. Follow the example of love, compassion, understanding and humility that Christ showed in His ministry. In this way your discipleship and service will be fruitful and effective, and fulfill its ultimate purpose of exalting God.

Master and Guide, I dedicate myself to You again, and offer my strength in Your service. Make me a joyful servant because I find my joy in You.

~ Amen ~

Rejoice in the Lord!

Then the people of Israel – the priests, the Levites and the rest of the exiles – celebrated the dedication of the house of God with joy. (Ezra 6:16)

Unfortunately, there are many people who associate worship with despondency, cheerlessness and even fear. Their attendance of church services is little more than habit. And they are tragically deprived of the greatest of all joys: joy in the Lord.

Through Christ, God invites you to receive the fullness of life that He offers you. As you turn to Him you become increasingly aware of His life-giving Spirit at work in you. Seemingly unattainable goals are suddenly within your reach; adversity does not overwhelm you because in Him you find the strength to overcome it; newly found confidence replaces your nervous pessimism. Day by day your faith grows stronger.

As you yield to the Holy Spirit, you will find that your worship, Bible study and prayer life gain new meaning. You will discover that God is not a vague, unreachable being, but an integral part of your life. Worship ought to be a joyful experience. Open yourself to the Holy Spirit, and He will raise you from despondency to joy in Christ.

O Holy Spirit, come into my life and fill me with the joy of the Lord.

~ Amen ~

Joyous Christianity

"My soul glorifies the Lord and my spirit rejoices in God my Savior." (Lk. 1:46-47)

Many people consider the Christian faith to be a heavy and sometimes even unbearable burden. They frown upon any semblance of light-heartedness in spiritual matters. They are oppressed by the heavy burden of their spiritual conscience. But God intended something far different for us.

Your Father delights in and is interested in your life. He is happy when you are happy; He consoles you when you are sad; He supports you when the burden becomes too heavy; He helps you up when you stumble over obstacles; He enjoys your successes as much as you do.

Christianity does not eliminate joy and happiness from life. On the contrary, it fills your life with abundant joy. Through fellowship with Christ you can know the blessing of His presence every day. The more you praise and thank Him, the more happiness you glean from life.

Joy is a fruit of the Holy Spirit (Gal. 5:22). Your faith and surrender to Christ should bring His joy to every area of our life.

Dear Lord Jesus, I continually delight in the knowledge that You are always with me.

~ Amen ~

DECEMBER 6

Our calling to cheerfulness

Rejoice in the Lord always. I will say it again: Rejoice!
(Phil. 4:4)

Christians are supposed to be cheerful, and if joy fills our lives, we will reap rich rewards spiritually. The world will also see that Christ has given us an indestructible joy that carries us through life. Many people spread gloom and doom wherever they go. But as a child of God, you can experience the joy and inspiration of the living Christ in your life, and so overcome moodiness and irritability.

When you are spiritually sensitive, you have no reason to be despondent. Your daily walk with Jesus Christ, the glorious promises in His Word and God's profound mercy will fill your life with joy, purpose and direction. If you live within the will of God, you can overcome frustration and truly appreciate all the blessings that God showers on you. Jesus redeemed you from sin with His blood. The Holy Spirit dwells in you! You are on your way "home". Just thinking of this sounds the death knell on all despondency.

Your cheerfulness is not a façade that you put up to impress people, but comes from a heart and mind that are in harmony with God through Jesus Christ.

Lord, You fill my days with joy. Your peace flows through me like a quiet stream. Even when I suffer, I know that You will deliver me.

~ Amen ~

Happiness in Christ

He who has clean hands and a pure heart, who does not lift up his soul to an idol or swear by what is false. He will receive blessing from the LORD and vindication from God his Savior. (Ps. 24:4-5)

No one can take away the joy and blessings that Christ gives us (see Jn. 16:22). We can find joy in Christ even when we are in pain. This joy cannot be erased by sorrow, loss, disappointment, or failure. It is a happiness that sees a rainbow through your tears.

Such joy emerges from an intimate walk with God: through each dark night, and every day ahead of us. It is like the ocean where waves toss and break on the surface but far below all is calm and quiet.

The joy that is found in Christ does not depend on our circumstances. It is a deep, everlasting, and steadfast joy. It is not something that we can strive for and attain through any human endeavor. It is a gift of God's grace.

The Holy Spirit will guide us and strengthen us to obey Christ, so that His happiness and blessing will become our portion.

Loving Master, thank You that the joy that You give is steadfast and indestructible, unlike the temporary and transient happiness of the world.

~ Amen ~

DECEMBER 8

Live like royal children

For you did not receive a spirit that makes you a slave again to fear, but you received the Spirit of sonship. And by him we cry, "Abba, Father." (Rom. 8:15)

There is a world of difference between confessing that you are a child of God and living as a child of God. Many people profess faith and yet live in constant fear. There is such a gap between what they should be and what they are that they tend to become despondent and abandon their faith.

When God called you to become His child and you joyfully responded to His call, a new life began for you. Your sins were forgiven and you entered a new relationship with the King. Through His grace you become a citizen of His kingdom. Because His Spirit now lives and works in you, your behavior toward people and your whole way of life have radically changed.

As we approach Christmas we are once again reminded that we should face life confidently and fearlessly. Your Father is the King of all kings. Knowing that He loves you and cares about you should give you inner peace. Steadfastly believing that He will guide you safely if you obey Him and love Him should be your comfort in life. Through Jesus Christ He invites you to call Him "Father".

Father, thank You that because of what Jesus Christ did on the cross, I can fellowship with You.

~ Amen ~

Christmas: feast of the child

She gave birth to her firstborn, a son. She wrapped him in cloths and placed him in a manger, because there was no room for them in the inn. (Lk. 2:7)

Every Christmas time we become children at heart once again. We relive the adventure of unquestioned faith, where all things are possible and where the child Jesus is in the center of everything. The stable becomes a palace and kings from the east kneel in worship before the King of kings.

For a short time we leave our mundane lives and wander down the paths of rich imagination, of wonder and delightful joy, while we freely rejoice in the infinite love of God. Even the staunchest realist finds his heart stirred when he hears the age-old tale of God's love.

The spirit of Christmas is also as real as the gifts that we exchange; as the candles we light; as the meals we share with family and loved ones; as the songs of praise that we hear everywhere at this wonderful time. As we experience the mystery of Christmas both tangibly and intangibly, we are touched by the wonder of God's love – and our dreams of peace and joy are rekindled.

I thank You, Lord Jesus, that I can enjoy the festivities surrounding Christmas with childlike glee and so enter into Your kingdom as a little child.

~ Amen ~

DECEMBER 10

The joy of Advent

"Say to the Daughter of Zion, 'See, your Savior comes! See, his reward is with him, and his recompense accompanies him.'" (Is. 62:11)

At Christmas time we commemorate Christ's coming into the world. But we must not forget that Christ has also come into our hearts and souls. He came as the Lamb of God to take the burden of sin and guilt from us. Celebrating Christmas without understanding its personal application to our lives sounds a false note in our lives.

All around us are outward expressions of celebration, but if we truly want to experience the joy of Christmas, Christ must bring His salvation into our hearts.

Christ came to fill the hearts of believers with love and grace. He came to find and save those who are lost, and everyone who accepts Him has the right to become children of God. He comes to turn your sadness into joy; He takes the false note of worldly celebration and replaces it with the true joy of Christmas.

Heavenly Father, we are once again on our annual pilgrimage to the manger in Bethlehem. Satisfy us with the true Bread and Water of life.

~ Amen ~

Feast for the world!

"Do not be afraid. I bring you good news of great joy that will be for all the people." (Lk. 2:10)

Many people are overwhelmed by a sense of unworthiness when they consider that Christ wants to come into their lives. Their understanding of Christianity causes such fear and anxiety that they turn away from Jesus.

Today, just as on the night of Jesus' birth more than 2 000 years ago, the angels bring us a message of "good news of great joy that will be for all the people". The presence of the living Christ in your heart will bring you the greatest joy that you could ever know.

The good news of Christmas is that Jesus Christ came to live with you. The angels promised that they had great news "for all people" – including you. Christ sacrificed Himself for you because of His great love, therefore you should not allow fear or anxiety to rob you of the opportunity to accept His offer to you. Get to know Him as Savior, Redeemer, Lord and Friend. Embrace Christ as the Lord of your life and experience the joy that the angels announced for all people.

Lord Jesus, Your coming into our broken world is the steadfast proof that God loves us and cares for us. We praise and thank You for that.

~ Amen ~

DECEMBER 12

The secret of a festive life

Always [give] thanks to God the Father for everything, in the name of our Lord Jesus Christ. (Eph. 5:20)

If Christ abides in you through faith, you develop a keener appreciation of the beauty and depth that are hidden in the lives of other people, as well as in the world around you.

If you, to the best of your ability, live in the Spirit, then you will develop insight and appreciation. The greater your gratitude, the more life will reveal its hidden treasures to you. Isaiah says Christ came, *"To comfort all who mourn, and provide for those who grieve in Zion – to bestow on them a crown of beauty instead of ashes, the oil of gladness instead of mourning, and a garment of praise instead of a spirit of despair"* (Is. 61:2-3).

It is important to be thankful. All through Scripture we hear the resounding echo of the praise of those who loved God and were grateful for His blessings. We appreciate the blessings, but we love God because He is our Father. He is infinitely patient and so merciful in His dealings with us. Our hearts overflow with gratitude for all He does for us.

Thank You, Lord Jesus, that Christmas reminds me that You have granted me Your love and gifts.

~ Amen ~

Can you truly celebrate Christmas?

Then they opened their treasures and presented him with gifts of gold and of incense and of myrrh. (Mt. 2:11).

The Magi understood the true meaning of Christmas: to give. At Christmas, God gave His best, His most valuable treasure – His Son. He gave out of love (see Jn. 3:16). And the Child of Bethlehem also gave: He gave Himself in His death on the cross.

Learn the secret of giving from giving. Forget what you did for others and remember what others did for you out of love. Rather than expecting things from others ask what you can do for them. Get rid of the idea that the world owes you something and think about what you owe the world.

As you become motivated by the gift that God gave to us at Christmas, you will become sensitive to people around you, people whose hearts yearn for love, friendship and compassion. Look around you to see where you can sow seeds of joy and kindness and love.

If you are willing to do these things then you will have brought your offering of gold, frankincense and myrrh to the Lord. And you will experience the true joy of Christmas.

Generous Lord, at this Christmas season, I once again offer my life to You to do with as You please.

~ Amen ~

God with us

DECEMBER 14

"They will call him Immanuel – which means, 'God with us.'" (Mt. 1:23)

Christmas teaches us the truth of sacrificial love. Christ came to His own people and they rejected Him, and yet He gave everyone who accepted Him the right to become children of God.

There was no room for Him in the inn, but He prepares a place in the Father's house for all who follow Him. He was despised and rejected, but He invites all who are weary and burdened to find rest in Him. He could have destroyed those who mocked Him, but He died on the cross so we could live forever. This is the meaning of Immanuel – God with us.

There is so much hatred in the world today. It poisons relationships between man and God, and between man and man. But Christmas reminds us that love will triumph. Because God is love, He sent us His Son. Because God loves us so much, we should also love one another. Let us profess our love anew this Christmas: to God, to our parents, to our spouses, to our children and to our fellowmen. Then Christmas will truly become a celebration.

Thank You, God of love, for allowing Your love to be embodied in Jesus Christ. Give us even more love through the work of the Holy Spirit.

~ Amen ~

Rejoice in the greatness of God

"My soul glorifies the Lord and my spirit rejoices in God my Savior, for he has been mindful of the humble state of his servant." (Lk. 1:46-48)

Many people believe that God is truly great and glorious, but their lifestyle contradicts their belief. Intellectually they accept the greatness of God, but the truth has not penetrated their hearts.

Many people call themselves Christians but live a life that is out of sync with the revelation of a great and mighty God. To fully appreciate His greatness, we need to acknowledge it in our spirits as well as in our minds. It is only when we begin to realize the greatness of God in our hearts that we begin to grow in the knowledge of Him.

God invites us to rejoice in the knowledge of Him, and in His greatness. And we should accept His invitation wholeheartedly. At this Christmas season, let the Holy Spirit reveal more of the greatness of God to you. Then His peace and joy will flood your heart.

The reality of His presence and the awareness of His indwelling Spirit make it possible for us to rejoice in the greatness of our God. Our Christmas carols should be filled with new meaning as we remember our great God.

Great and Holy God, give me a clear understanding of Your greatness so that I can truly rejoice in my salvation.

~ Amen ~

Take a break

DECEMBER 16

"In repentance and rest is your salvation, in quietness and trust is your strength, but you would have none of it." (Is. 30:15)

Many people take a much-needed break from the demands of jobs and careers over Christmas. It is good to leave the rat race behind for a while. It is not easy to become quiet in our noisy world, which is why we need to strive to enter the rest of God. Slowing down over the holidays helps us achieve this.

As we withdraw from the confusion of daily life and spend time in nature, we once again connect with God. Our tension eases with the soothing rhythm of mountain streams and the incessant song of the sea.

Slow down and enjoy the things that we let slip in the everyday rush of the rest of the year: long conversations with family members; the beauty of creation; the delight in a child's eyes; playing with pets; and, most of all, digging deep into the Word of God. Look up into the branches of tall trees, and remember that they grow slowly. Allow God to bring His refreshing strength into your life again, and accept His gifts of peace and joy.

Creator God, thank You for restoring Your peace to me in times of quietness and rest.

~ Amen ~

Christmas meditation

The Word became flesh and made his dwelling among us. We have seen his glory, the glory of the One and Only, who came from the Father, full of grace and truth. (Jn. 1:14)

As we prayerfully meditate on the awesome miracle of Christ's birth, let us once again pledge to:

- Make Christ the central focus of our celebrations. Let us honor Him in our hearts and in our actions.
- Avoid being dragged into the commercialization of Christmas. We should refuse to participate in the mad rush and wanton excess that occurs at Christmas time. Let us not get so caught up in the shiny tinsel and other trappings of Christmas that we lose sight of the Babe in the manger.
- Remember that Christmas is a time for families to be together. Let us not seek our Christmas joy in frivolous and worldly pleasures but in the warmth and intimacy of our home, where Christ is also always welcome.
- Join our family in the House of God on Christmas morning.
- Let every Christmas card we send bear witness to our faith in Christ.
- Nurture the true spirit of Christmas in our children's hearts. And then the fullness of Christmas joy will be with us all through the year.

Jesus of Nazareth, help me to approach Christmas with a pure heart and the right attitude.

~ Amen ~

Fulfillment in Christ

December 18

As the deer pants for streams of water, so my soul pants for you, O God. My soul thirsts for God, for the living God. (Ps. 42:1-2)

The same longing that moved the psalmist's heart is evident in the hearts of people today. People have the same longing to know God but they disguise it behind "psychobabble" because they do not want to admit their failings and weaknesses. But they will never find daily happiness apart from God.

They spend their lives searching for satisfaction and joy, while wandering blindly along paths that they imagine to be real. They fill their lives with a searching after material possessions or prestige or power, but find no joy or satisfaction. They neglect spiritual values, dismissing those who value spiritual things as foolish fanatics.

But those who are truly wise know that true satisfaction and fulfillment are to be found only in spiritual things. A proper balance between material and spiritual aspects of life must be maintained, and this is only possible when Christ is at the center of your life.

The Lord cares about every aspect of your life, and when you taste and see that He is good, your life will be rich and fruitful.

Living Savior, in You alone I find fulfillment and satisfaction. Praise Your holy name.

~ Amen ~

A vision from God

"Let's go to Bethlehem and see this thing that has happened, which the Lord has told us about." (Lk. 2:15)

The shepherds were amazed when they saw the angels of God and the glory of the heavens that first Christmas night. They immediately responded to the vision that God had shown them. They did not first confer with a committee or set up a commission of enquiry into the matter. They simply said, "Let us go to Bethlehem."

All those who follow the Lord can experience the reality of His presence and be deeply touched by the wonders of His love. Such experiences seem almost too holy to share with others, but the danger is that we keep them hidden in our hearts, and eventually they fade from memory.

If God has revealed Himself to you in a special way, then He has a specific purpose for you to fulfill. He may have filled your heart with a burning love for others or have called you to tell others of the joy He gives. At Christmas, we are reminded of the holy and inspired visions through which God has revealed to us all that He intends us to be.

Lord Jesus, give me the courage and wisdom to respond to the vision You have for my life.

~ Amen ~

Christ-feast!

"Do not be afraid. I bring you good news of great joy that will be for all the people." (Lk. 2:10)

The world has eliminated Christ from the festivities of Christmas to make room for worldly pleasures. As Christians, we need to rectify this travesty.

We must guard against the commercialization of Christmas that so dishonors God. Christmas must not be allowed to degenerate into cheap tinsel, shining lights and superficial emotions.

We must not be swept up in the mad rush before Christmas and be left so exhausted on Christmas Day that we are unable to sing songs of praise in His honor. We must look beneath the trappings and uncover the core of Christmas, letting the Light of the world shine in our lives.

Christians have more reason to celebrate Christmas than other people do. We should celebrate with the angels who appeared in the fields of Bethlehem and filled the sky with joy on that holy night long ago. Without Christ there can be no true Christmas joy.

The true glory of Christmas is to be found in our hearts, not in shopping malls and worldly parties. Let the world see in us the true spirit of Christmas so that they too can come and worship the King.

Holy Spirit of God, this Christmas guide me past the external trappings to the true inner joy that can only be found in Christ.

~ Amen ~

The humble host of the feast

And there were shepherds living out in the fields nearby, keeping watch over their flocks at night. (Lk. 2:8)

The emperor and the governor did not hear of it; Herod and the chief priests were not aware of it; but God sent His angels to simple shepherds with the message: the Prince of Peace has been born in a stable in Bethlehem! No trumpet proclaimed that the Son of God had been born. The greatest event in history occurred without publicity or fanfare.

Christ's advent into the world was typical of His life and ministry. The Host of heaven lived a quiet and simple life on earth. The first to know about it were the poor, the illiterate, the shepherds who lived in the fields and watched over their flocks in the cold winter night. In these events we see the humility and simplicity that characterized all that Jesus did on earth.

Allow God to transform you into the image of Christ, so that, in this festive season and throughout the year, you will reflect His character and so bring peace and joy into our sin-torn world.

Preserve me from pride Lord, and help me make You welcome in my heart.

~ Amen ~

DECEMBER 22

How will you prepare for the feast?

For to us a child is born, to us a son is given ... And he will be called Wonderful Counselor, Mighty God, Everlasting Father, Prince of Peace. (Is. 9:6)

People all over the world are preparing for the "holiday season". Christmas is coming. Families indulge in spending sprees and everyone anticipates the large-scale pleasure, joy and merry-making that abound at this time of year.

While we enjoy such activities we must not forget that it is also the blessed time of Advent. It is a time in which to prepare ourselves, not for parties or shopping expeditions, but to celebrate because the Savior of the world was born. We want to celebrate this miracle with joy, and with holy zeal. We must reflect on the reason for His coming to this sin-filled world. We must once again examine our spiritual life humbly before God, asking Him to make us worthy, through the work of His Holy Spirit, to live with Him.

It is an overwhelming thought that God took it upon Himself to come and live amongst us as a man. May this be the foremost thought in your heart and in your celebrations during the Christmas season.

Holy Jesus, prepare our hearts so that we will celebrate Christmas in a worthy manner.

~ Amen ~

Festive season of the soul

"Today in the town of David a Savior has been born to you; he is Christ the Lord." (Lk. 2:11)

The world is filled with the sounds of Christmas. You can hear festive songs, bells, laughter and, now and again, a sob of sorrow and loneliness. But if you listen with your soul, you will hear the angels singing, the joy of anticipation and the sanctified sound of holy silence. You will hear the whisper of the Eternal Word that became Flesh in Jesus Christ.

The world is filled with the symbols of Christmas. You can see gift-laden trees telling a story of love and joy, bright golden stars, burning candles and a manger. But if you look with the eyes of your heart, you will see the Star of Bethlehem in your own heart; you will see the radiant glory of Christ's presence, reborn in you when you portray His love.

Christmas is a continuous season of the soul, and Bethlehem lives forever in your heart. Through God's grace, the eyes and the ears of your heart will be opened and you will hear the joyful sounds of celebration because of the Word that came to live among us.

Savior and Friend of sinners, thank You for this season of the soul when we can listen to the soundless Word that became flesh.

~ Amen ~

DECEMBER 24

A star shines in Bethlehem

When they saw the star, they were overjoyed. (Mt. 2:10)

Christmas brings a feeling of joy, goodwill and peace to our hearts. Ever since Christ was born in Bethlehem, people all over the world have experienced the joy of His coming, regardless of the way the world has changed.

Jesus came to bring light to this dark world. The light of the star guided people to the manger so that they could joyfully behold their Savior. The Star of Bethlehem still lights your path through the darkness of temptation and wickedness, to bring you to the path that leads to God. There, in a stable in a little bed of straw, you see how God, through the eyes of a baby, invites people to return to Him.

During this festive season and as you approach the new year, fix your eyes upon the Savior of the world. He is your Guiding Star and will lead you to peace and goodwill. *"This is the message we have heard from him and declare to you: God is light; in him there is no darkness at all."* (1 Jn. 1:5). He is the bright Morning Star.

Morning Star, thank You for leading me on the path that leads to eternal life.

~ Amen ~

Christ is born!

DECEMBER 25

Jesus was born in Bethlehem in Judea, during the time of King Herod. (Mt. 2:1)

It is an irrefutable historical fact that Jesus was born in Bethlehem. Through this physical birth God revealed Himself to all of humanity.

The One who was born in Bethlehem more than two thousand years ago is still being born in the hearts and lives of people today. But in the busyness of our lives we often lose sight of this truth.

In spite of the world's festivities around Christmas time, if you have not experienced the birth of Christ in your heart, you will never know the true joy and peace of Christmas. Only Christ gives depth and peace to the joy of Christmas. The birth of Christ in Bethlehem is nothing more than a historical fact until He is born in your life. Then you will know not only Christmas, but also the Christ of Christmas.

If you want to experience true Christmas joy, Christ must be born in your life and be given the place of honor in your life – the very center of it. When His holiness permeates your life, it becomes "a merry Christmas" in the true sense of the word.

I thank You, holy Child of Bethlehem, for being born in me so that I can partake of Your Spirit, and so that my entire life can be a celebration in Your honor.

~ Amen ~

Feast of hope

DECEMBER 26

Always be prepared to give an answer to everyone who asks you to give the reason for the hope that you have. (1 Pet. 3:15)

Centuries have passed since the birth of Christ, and, regardless of a stubborn, disobedient and loveless world, He is still the same Savior. God became man, and was born in a humble stable in Bethlehem but man still tramples on the truth in order to achieve his own selfish ends.

As the year hurtles to a close we would have been tempted to lose hope altogether, but the blessed Feast of Christ reminds us that Jesus came to this world to save sinners. Regardless of the despondency and despair surrounding us, a beacon of love shines – the Light of the world invites us to leave the darkness behind, put our hope in Him and face the future with hope in our hearts.

Christmas should remind us that, in spite of the suffering we endure, and regardless of what is threatening us, Christ is our hope for the future, as He has been for His children through the ages. We have the assurance in our hearts that nothing can separate us from the love of God in Christ Jesus. In this hope we celebrate.

Lord Jesus of Bethlehem, thank You that You came to place hope in our hearts and our lives.

~ Amen ~

Cheerful givers

God loves a cheerful giver. (2 Cor. 9:7)

Because God gave us the great gift of His Son, we give each other gifts at Christmas. A gift given graciously and with joy, increases and enriches its value. It is the duty and privilege of every Christian to be a giver. When the Holy Spirit of the living Christ flows through you, He teaches you to love and withhold nothing that will bless and enrich your neighbor. Your purpose in life is to be a blessing to others.

Let each gift be accompanied by a desire that God will bless the one who receives it, and be thankful that you are able to give. Remember that giving money or possessions is not the most important gift that you can offer. God has given you a personality that you should develop to His glory in the service of others. To be cheerful, in the Name of Jesus, is to be like a ray of light that breaks through a dark bank of clouds. Every Christian can give the gift of a cheerful and hopeful heart to others.

God gives freely, without any obligations, and you and I should do the same.

You gave us Your Son, O Father. Grant that we will give ourselves unconditionally to You.

~ Amen ~

DECEMBER 28

A Christian character

"But we know that when he appears, we shall be like him, for we shall see him as he is." (1 Jn. 3:2)

Every Christian should endeavor to build his life according to the pattern of Christ's life. This will vary according to our personalities, but the all-embracing desire should be to grow into conformity with Christ.

Yielding to the lordship of Christ is the beginning of a new and enriching way of life. Of course, it is impossible to perfect this pattern through your own efforts. Trying to do this in your own strength will only lead to frustration and disappointment. When you accept Christ as the Lord of your life, He becomes a reality to you. If you ask Him, He will give you His Holy Spirit. When you are united with Him, your faith starts to come alive and you find the ability to obey Him cheerfully.

From this obedience, a Christlike character develops. It is wonderful to note that people who have learned to be like Christ are not usually aware of it in themselves. People who are conformed to Christ are too busy loving their fellowmen. Their holiness is a by-product of their fellowship with their Master.

Lord, at the end of the year my heart is so full, and I want to dedicate myself to You again as the new year approaches. Conform me to Your image.

~ Amen ~

Year-end meditation

So do not fear, for I am with you; do not be dismayed, for I am your God. I will strengthen you and help you, I will uphold you with my righteous right hand. (Is. 41:10)

As the year draws to a close, we tend to look back at what has been. Unfortunately, for many people this means focusing on failures, disappointments and setbacks and so they face the future with fear.

There is a place for looking back at the past but it must be constructive. Learn how to use your past, mistakes for your advantage instead of groaning under their burden. Similarly, when you think about the successes of the past, it is no excuse to rest on your laurels. They should inspire you to reach even greater heights.

After you have reviewed the events of the past year, you should resolve to face the new year in intimate fellowship with the living Christ. Allow Him to be your Counselor and Guide. Let your heart be sensitive to the whisperings of the Holy Spirit and resolve to obey Him unconditionally.

Then you can rest assured that, regardless of what happens in your life, you can face the future with confidence, filled with the peace that comes from God alone.

Eternal God, thank You for the assurance at the end of this year that You are always with us and that You will hold us in Your hand.

~ Amen ~

New life in Christ

DECEMBER 30

Examine yourselves to see whether you are in the faith; test yourselves. Do you not realize that Christ Jesus is in you – unless, of course, you fail the test? (2 Cor. 13:5)

The great stabilizing factor in the Christian life is the fact that Christ lives in us. It doesn't depend on how you feel and what you do, on your opinions or your emotions. Jesus Christ is in the hearts of those who acknowledge His lordship, who love Him with all their might and who serve Him to the best of their ability.

The glorious truth that Christ lives in you should revolutionize your life. You will see other people in a new light, as kindred spirits involved in the great adventure of living. When Christ lives in you, your view of life is enriched. This creates a broader vision and a spiritual depth and perception that help you to understand more about the world and God.

Christ not only gives you a fresh approach to life, but also supplies you with the inner strength that enables you to live victoriously. He gives you all you need for an inspired, goal-directed, satisfying life. Because Christ lives in you, your whole life becomes a new, exciting and satisfying experience.

I praise and thank You, Lord Jesus for all Your grace in the year that has past, and the hope that You give me for the future.

~ Amen ~

Epilogue: grace inconceivably great

So is my word that goes out from my mouth: It will not return to me empty, but will accomplish what I desire and achieve the purpose for which I sent it. (Is. 55:11)

O Lord, my God, I praise Your holy Name. Your love knows no bounds! May Your precious words fill my thoughts and life. Let me always hold firmly onto Your hand and so inherit Your kingdom.

Thank You for comforting me when I am mourning, so that I can see rainbows through my tears. Thank You for placing a hunger and thirst for righteousness in my soul, so that I can live well and do good each day. Help me always to have compassion for others, so that I can truly serve them in love. Then I will not fail to find Your mercy.

Create in me a pure heart, O God, so that my eyes can see Your glory. I so want to live as Your child. Enable me to be a peacemaker.

Lord, my God and Father, make me the salt of the earth and a light of the world as I serve You, so that Your name may be glorified in my life. I ask for all this through the blood of Jesus, my Savior and Redeemer.

~ Amen ~